Kendal Br

THE HISTORY OF KENDAL
AND SNUFF INDU

~

J.W. Dunderdale

Edited by
Anne Bonney

Congratulations on reaching 'Old Git' status

Best Wishes
Tel.

HELM
PRESS

With acknowledgement to the assistance
of the Curwen Archive Trust

Dedicated to my family and the people of Kendal

Published by Helm Press
10 Abbey Gardens, Natland, Kendal, Cumbria LA9 7SP
Tel: 015395 61321
E-mail: HelmPress@natland.freeserve.co.uk

First published 2003

Typeset in Minion

ISBN 0 9540497 5 6

Typeset and printed by
MTP Media Ltd, The Sidings, Beezon Fields, Kendal. Cumbria LA9 6BL

Front cover: Sorting and preparing tobacco leaves proir to making twist

CONTENTS

INTRODUCTION vii

1. **HISTORIC BACKGROUND TO SNUFF** 9

2. **KENDAL AND SNUFF** 13

3. **SAMUEL GAWITH & COMPANY** 25
   Thomas Harrison's foray into Scotland 25
   Earliest Snuff Manufacturing Plant 25
   Mealbank Mill 27
   Brocklebank and Harrison – early beginnings 29
   Lowther Street premises 30
   Samuel Gawith 31
   Brocklebank & Gawith, Tobacco and Snuff Manufacturers 32
   Trustees 34
   Samuel the Second and John Edward Gawith – Tobacco and Snuff Manufacturers 35
   An Agreement of Separation 37
   Kendal Brown House 38
   John Edward Gawith 38
   Samuel Gawith the Second 41
   Albert Philipson and John Rigg – Mealbank 43
   Samuel Gawith the Second – the man 43
   Samuel Gawith the Third 45
   Mr W. Pennington 48
   The Workers 51
   Transport 51
   Bladders used for storing snuff 51
   Westmorland Gazette 14 March 1903 51
   Sandes Avenue Factory – 1920 'The Tobacco Factory' Kendal 55
   Takeover of Messrs Wm Nevinson's, Eamont Bridge 56
   Snuff Production only – Kendal Brown House 56
   Eamont Bridge Mill closure – 1937 60
   Picture Cards 60
   List of Samuel Gawith workers 62

Douglas Harris 66
Mrs D. M. Dakeyne-Cannon 69
Four Mortar Snuff Grinding Mill – oldest operational in the country 70
'Jumbo' from Eamont Bridge 71
The Firm in 2003 71
Snuff Mill today 73
Essence room 75

4. ILLINGWORTH'S 77
John Thomas Illingworth 77
Dr Rumney 78
Marriage to Catharine Rumney 79
The Children 80
Drug Store Yard 80
Extended Premises in Highgate 81
J. T. Illingworth & Sons 82
John Thomas dies 83
George Rumney Illingworth leaves 83
James marriage to Mary Agnes Butterwith 83
Airecliffe 84
Messrs John T. Illingworth & Sons 84
Sandes Avenue Factory 84
Bonded Warehouse 86
Cigarette Production 88
New 'Ten Packs' – cigarette cards – to boost sales 88
Fancy Packet Tobaccos 89
1914–18 Surge in demand 90
Larger Premises – Aynam Mills 90
Now next door to Samuel Gawith & Co. 92
Card details 93
Sale of tobacco/cigarette side to Robinson & Sons of Stockport 95
Snuff Mill (Little Aynam end) – Illingworths Snuffs Ltd – 1929 96
John Harold Thomas – managing director 96
James Rumney Illingworth – the man 97
Robinson's taken over by Gallahers – more cards 100
Gallahers issue cards for the popular Illingworth's No 10 103
Singleton & Cole Ltd 103
Illingworth's supplying raw snuff or snuff flour to Singleton's 104

Robert Cottam 106
Illlingworth's acquired by Leo Waddington
and sold onto Singleton & Cole Ltd 106
Illingworth's Snuffs Ltd – 1964 become wholly owned
subsidiary of Singleton & Cole Ltd 107
Cavenhams takeover – Illingworth's Tobaccos Ltd 108
Ceased dealing in cigarettes in 1972 109
Trade Mark – coloured rooster on a reclining crescent moon 110
Mill 112
The Fire 112
New Factory 114
Takeover by J. & H. Wilson 116
Closure 116

5. GAWITH, HOGGARTH & COMPANY 117
William Henry Gawith and Henry Hoggarth Jnr 117
Background 119
The two Henry's the founders 120
27 Lowther Street 121
Both employed or re-employed by Samuel Gawith Co 123
Founding of Gawith, Hoggarth in 1887 123
27 Lowther St – possibly rented for a time
by Samuel Gawith & Co 123
Acquired the business of Noble & Wilson 124
Woolpack Yard 126
Natland Beck Mill 127
Helsington Laithes Mill 129
William Henry Gawith's marriage to Harriet Hoggarth 131
27 Lowther Street – becomes factory and office to
Gawith, Hoggarth & Co 1893 132
William Henry Gawith died 1895 132
Samuel Henry Gawith 135
Gawith, Hoggarth & Co 1923 – Limited Liability Company 138
Henry Hoggarth – civil duties 139
Christmas Gifts 1914–18 War 139
Henry Hoggarth died in 1928 140
Samuel Henry Gawith – Chairman, Frank D. Hoggarth
– Director, Charles E. Hoggarth – Director 142
Samuel Henry Gawith and his family 143

Geoffrey Francis Gawith 144
Doris Hoggarth (temporary secretary during husband's wartime absence) 144
Shake ups and retirements 144
Samuel Henry Gawith died in 1966 145
Geoffrey F. Gawith – Chairman 1966 145
Mrs M. T. Gawith takes over as temporary secretary 146
Further moves and promotions 146
Charles E. Hoggarth retires in 1973 147
Sole owners in 1980 – Geoffrey F. and John R. Gawith 147
Firm's premises, plant and products 147
Countries tobacco comes from 148
Tobacco categories 149
Blending 149
Manufacture of twist 150
Trade Signs – 'Turk' 151
Helsington Snuff Mill 152
Blending, perfuming and packaging of snuff at Lowther Street 157
Variations in snuff 157
The Last Miller 157
The firm in 2003 167

REFERENCES 173

Introduction

THE AUTHOR JAMES WILLIAM DUNDERDALE was born on 23 September 1912 in Mansfield, Nottinghamshire, and was educated at King Edward School. He later worked as a precision engineer for Bowman and Turners. James married on 31 July 1937 to Elsie and they had a daughter Patricia in 1941. The family moved to Southport in 1957 where they bought and ran a Nursing Home. In 1979 they retired to Kendal and lived at 128 Burneside Road.

James had collected cigarette cards since he was a boy of ten and had amassed a large collection. He also had a keen interest in local history and was fascinated to find out that of the six firms that manufactured snuff in the United Kingdom, three of them should be based in Kendal and that little had been written about them apart from newspaper and magazine articles. James decided he had to find out more about them and meticulously researched the history of tobacco and snuff in Kendal.

It was completed about 1980 but unfortunately was never published at the time. James sadly died on 8 January 1996 and is survived by his widow, and married daughter, who now live in Worcester.

Two years ago, when his daughter was still living in Kendal she showed her father's article to a friend and then in turn to me. The manuscript ends with the three snuff firms in 1980. A lot of work has gone into the research and upon reading it I decided that it should be published but further work had to be done.

I have edited James' work as well as adding further information that has come to light, together with bringing the history of the firms up to present day. I have also interviewed some of the employees both past and present as well as introducing some of their stories.

I would like to thank the management and staff of the two surviving snuff firms and the ex-employees of the late Illingworth's firm together with family members both past and present, who helped me either orally or by lending photographs and paraphernalia, encouragement and support. Thank you also to members of staff in the Local Studies Section, at

James Dunderdale with his wife, Elsie

Kendal Library and staff at the Kendal Record Office. I would particularly like to thank Geoff Thompson, who from the outset has been outstanding and unstinting with his knowledge and help throughout.

Finally, I must add that whilst every effort has made to trace all copyright holders of the photographs used, I apologise to any holders I have not acknowledged and would be grateful if I could be notified of any correction to be incorporated in any future edition. I have also tried to make it as accurate as possible, so please forgive me if I have made any slight errors along the way.

With the help of many people this book on the history of snuff has come to life so please read on and enjoy just one of things that Kendal is renowned for throughout the world.

Anne Bonney
July 2003

ONE

Historic Background to Snuff

THERE WERE, IN 1980, ONLY SIX FIRMS in the whole of the British Isles making snuff (that is milling the snuff from the raw tobacco and finishing it ready for sale) and that three out of these six should be located in one town is something unique. The other English town renowned for producing snuff is Sheffield and this remains to this day. To the best of my knowledge nowhere else in the world are there to be found three snuff mills in one town, but then Kendal is a unique place.

From earliest times Kendal has been a manufacturing centre/town, a place where produce, and local produce in particular, has been treated and finished ready for sale, and, be it noted, in the past some of Kendal's products have been famous, and as such sold all over this country and even abroad.

Kendal and the Kent Basin had first corn, then fulling mills, and much later, in the first half of the nineteenth century, a proliferation of watermills, for by then machinery had been designed to produce many and varied articles and we had the peak of the first, the water powered, industrial revolution. This seeded early with the corn and the fulling mills, blossomed slowly during the seventeenth and eighteenth centuries, fruited quickly during the first half of the nineteenth century, and died rapidly in the last half of that century, with the arrival of steam power. But that peak of the waterpower age in the early years of the nineteenth century saw the second peak of Kendal's industrial prosperity. For in the by then reduced but still extensive parish of Kendal there were over forty water driven mills producing a wide range of goods, while the number of such mills in the Kent Basin as a whole was estimated to be about ninety. A figure like this meant that the Kendal area was the most heavily industrialised one in England, at that time, having something like one mill to every three hundred and fifty people. By comparison Birmingham having at that time a ratio of one mill to over one thousand people.

From the foregoing it will be seen that by the time tobacco was introduced into the scene in this country, say 1600, Kendal was a thriving commercial centre with water driven production capacity and a skilled labour force.

The 'weed' was first introduced into Europe via Spain and Portugal, and there, by those who accompanied first Columbus and then the Spanish and the Portuguese *Conquistadors*. Then, from Spain, the use of tobacco spread across the Pyrenees to France. By the middle of the sixteenth century snuff making was well established there. Two Frenchmen were chiefly responsible for introducing and establishing the use of tobacco into France. The first was André Thevet. A little later Jean Nicot, the French Ambassador to the Portuguese Court, who grew tobacco in France and praised and extolled its use as a healing and health-giving herb, really clinched it. Here is not the time or place to detail the history of the use of tobacco and snuff in Europe but it is sufficient to say that most European countries, and Scotland adopted the use of tobacco first via the medium of snuff in the sixteenth century. They called it 'sneshing' and called snuff boxes 'mulls'. In England alone was the smoking of tobacco followed by snuff making.

These first supposed cures were greeted with great enthusiasm in France, and it was here that the plant was named 'nicotina' in honour of its champion, hence, nicotine, the essence, the be all and end all of tobacco in any form.

It is not always recognised today that up to at least the year 1700 and in many cases even later, tobacco was credited as being the universal 'cure all'. Medical men and apothecaries maintained that tobacco was a medicine and one that they prescribed in many and various forms. These forms included poultices, distilled tobacco juice, powdered ash, chewing, as well as snuff and smoking by pipe. Incidentally these same physicians and apothecaries were the first preparers of tobacco for sale, either as snuff or as pipe tobacco.

Tobacco as a thing to be smoked, was introduced into England only at the end of the sixteenth century, by men such as Drake and Raleigh. It was a costly luxury, the selling price in these early days was fixed by its 'wayte in silver', so that 'smoking' only caught on really with the wealthy. Smoking then required wealth, leisure, and, at all times, a handy fire, three things in short supply in working class circles, in which the men spent little time at home apart from sleeping, and, with regard to the last point, try 'lighting up' even today in a field without matches or lighter!

Then, in 1604, King James I came down firmly on smoking with his famous 'Counterblaste to Tobacco', a Royal Manifesto, with his cruel increases in taxation. He raised the tobacco duty from two pence per

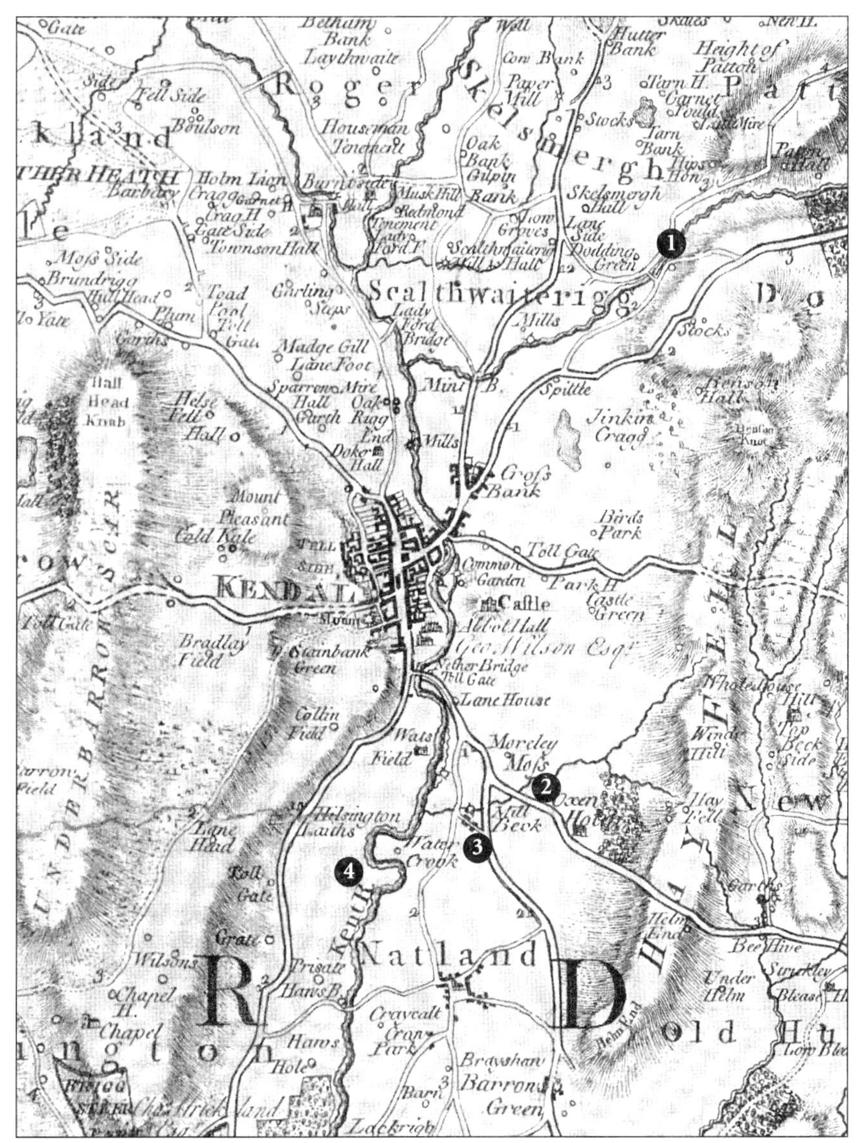

Thomas Jeffreys map of Westmorland 1770 showing the mills around Kendal.

Key:

1 Mealbank
2 Snuff Mill Meadow (Close)
3 Natland Beck Mill
4 Helsington Mill

pound, to six shillings and ten pence per pound, a rise of four thousand per cent, which, incidentally, started tobacco smuggling. His hatred of tobacco in any form was virulent. These measures, to which were added others, such as a 1619 decree prohibiting the growing of tobacco in England, taken together with the then current fashion in genteel society for imitating French Court manners (with both Louis XIII and Louis XIV snuff addicts), succeeded in converting the English to a snuff taking nation, as were already most of the other countries of Europe. Remember that tobacco as snuff is cheaper, a pinch as against a bowl full, is, by its very nature, easier and more convenient to take, and in addition delivers, ounce for ounce, more nicotine than smoking tobacco.

The snuff boom in England really took off in the year 1700 with Admiral Sir George Rooke's 'bounty'. The story is briefly thus. He and his ships intercepted and spoiled a Spanish treasure fleet on its way home from the Spanish Americas carrying amongst other things thousands of small kegs of best quality snuff. The greater part of this snuff hoard was distributed amongst the crews of the English ships as bounty, one keg per man. Now most of this fine snuff found its way, via many different home ports and all kinds of outlets, to many old and, because of the cheapness of its bounty price, to many new, or first time, snuff takers. The net result was that all of the sailors did well financially, even though they sold off their bounty extremely cheaply in most cases, snuff was introduced to a wide new market, and many of the purchasers became 'hooked'. Soon after this it was reported that there were in London alone over one thousand shops where snuff was sold.

TWO

Kendal and Snuff

Kendal benefited from this boom because by then the tobacco and snuff industry had become established in the town, a number of later to be noted developments contributing to the growth of this new industry. First let us go back a hundred years and take a look at the birth of the industry in Kendal, that I have given as being around 1623. It stems, I believe, from the following episode in the town's, and tobacco's history. The sixteenth and early seventeenth century was a time of pestilence and of plague in this country, and in 1598 the plague struck Kendal so grievously that two thousand five hundred inhabitants died. The plague struck the town again in 1623 but this visit resulted in a much lighter death toll. Now in between the two above dates the medicinal benefits of tobacco had become widely circulated and believed in (tobacco was called the 'herba panacea' and it was especially advocated as a disinfectant, or a safeguard against infection, in addition to being recommended as a remedy for ills ranging from toothache to colds and one to be used liberally, on the premise that prevention was better than cure), and the mildness of the second plague attack was attributed in no small part to the use by the townspeople of tobacco, and in particular to snuff.

The events above resulted in a strong local demand for snuff and tobacco, while circumstances of time and place provided a soil favourable for the growth of an industry to meet this demand. At this time, around 1623, tobacco was beginning to be grown in the British Colonies of Virginia and Maryland as a valuable export crop, the quantity of leaf shipped from Virginia alone rising by 1629 to one and a half million pounds. At the same time, or beginning at the same time, mainly to cope with this growing American trade, the Cumberland coastal ports such as Whitehaven had entered a period of steady expansion. Having had only a small coal pier built in 1634, the harbour was later extended by Sir John Lowther to facilitate the coal trade with Ireland. The port steadily grew and following a local sea captain's voyage to America in 1675 came the first interest in tobacco.

Lithograph of Whitehaven Harbour 1844.
The Beacon, Whitehaven – Copeland Borough Council

Kendal, because of its nearness to these ports, and by the fact that it lay on the direct route into England from both the Cumberland Ports and also from Glasgow, (to become by 1700 the major snuff and tobacco manufacturing centre of Britain) was in a very favourable position. Through its nationwide woollen cloth trade, other trades, such as tanning, leather and shoe, the town had built up a network of customer connections and transport routes and facilities rivalled by few at that time. Again, for this new trade, a uniquely available supply of its raw material, tobacco leaf (for all the shipments of this commodity landed at the Cumberland Ports and destined for ninety per cent of the English market had to pass through it) was readily available to the town. As Kendal was just one full days' journey (in that day) from the Cumberland Ports, and the first staging post (with often a change of horses), much of all the merchandise, tobacco included, was, naturally, dropped off here. After all why cart it further if you could leave some of it and some of your beasts here and then pick up on your way back these same animals loaded with Kendal goods for shipment? So Kendal had the pick of the crop. Again, in a time of a Colonial shortage etc Kendal had the alternative advantage of being in a similar situation with Glasgow, being able to trade with the tobacco houses there, which Kendalians did, and also took advantage of Scottish know-how, as will be seen later.

With regard to the Cumberland Ports, Whitehaven, Workington, Maryport, etc, these, became during the seventeenth and the eighteenth centuries more and more important as the American trade grew. As in the case of Kendal, several factors combined to bring about the rise of these towns of which Whitehaven was typical. One factor was Whitehaven's nearness of landfall to the Americas, and another, and important one, was its distance away from British southern waters and ports. For this was an age of maritime warfare between England and the Continent and the era of the 'privateer', Dutch, French or Spanish, to whom all shipping was fair game. Ships had to be well acquitted for this, indeed the 'Friendship' on her 1761 tobacco voyage, carried 18 guns and a crew of 28 men. In Whitehaven's case the resultant growth of trade was such that by 1772 the tonnage of British ships cleared from the port was over twice that from Liverpool in the same year, and in 1799 no less than two hundred and sixteen merchant ships were registered at Whitehaven. The import of raw tobacco and the re-export of finished tobaccos and snuffs formed a major part of the trade, witness the fact that as early as 1739–40 the port is credited with importing four and a half million pounds of tobacco. The port even had its own Customs Officers and was no longer tied to the Port of Carlisle.

The Glaswegian merchants had established direct links with the Colonies in 1665, but tobacco imports were forbidden by the 1671 Navigation Act, unless they first passed through an English port. Glaswegians overcame this problem by using Whitehaven ships. This later changed with the union with Scotland in 1707 and was a severe blow to the English tobacco trade. There were ups and downs,

Above: Ships bowl made of Liverpool Delftware circa 1744 to commemorate the Whitehaven vessel 'Love', which was used in the America tobacco trade.

Friends of Whitehaven Museum

whereby the Glaswegian merchants did not have enough ships and had to employ the Cumberland masters once again. There was a further hiccup in trade over money and alleged customs frauds between the Glasgow and Whitehaven merchants. Whitehaven's tobacco trade exploded in the 1730s and 1740s with the exploitation of the European markets of Holland and France, which led to anything up to half the tobacco being re-exported at this time.

By the end of the eighteenth century much of this tobacco trade was lost to Glasgow, where, during the century many tobacco warehouses together with blending and processing plants had been established, and where these last included the first water driven snuff mills of the British Islands.

This change was not altogether detrimental to Kendal, as much of the Glasgow output was destined for the English market, and Kendal lay on the direct pack horse (later wagon) road, or track (as it first was), into England deriving from this the same advantages as was the case with the Whitehaven connection.

The mention of roads and, or, pack horse tracks highlights another very important factor that contributed much to Kendal's success as an industrial town. It has to be remembered that prior to the establishment of the Turnpike Trusts, roads for wheeled traffic between towns were practically non-existent in Britain in general, and this was especially so in the Lake District. The first 'made' road in our area and for at least thirty miles around was a stretch from Kendal to Keighley, for strange as it may seem to us today, the then main route (pack horse track before road) from Kendal to London went that way, passing through Preston Patrick, Kirkby Lonsdale, Skipton and Keighley on its way south. The Trust for this road was formed by an Act of Parliament in 1752, and the making of the road commenced the same year. Before this the carriage of goods between towns had been by pack horse over pack horse tracks, these last being nobodies business when it came to maintenance and repair. Even after this and the other trunk and turnpike roads had been made, it was years before the pack horse was altogether superseded by wagons and coaches.

Kendal, with regard to the pack horse traffic, was a kind of pre railway Crewe Junction, where teams met and loads were exchanged, in addition to being a staging post and over night stop for the long distance teams passing through. It has been computed that some three hundred and fifty pack horses carried goods in and out of Kendal every week, the teams

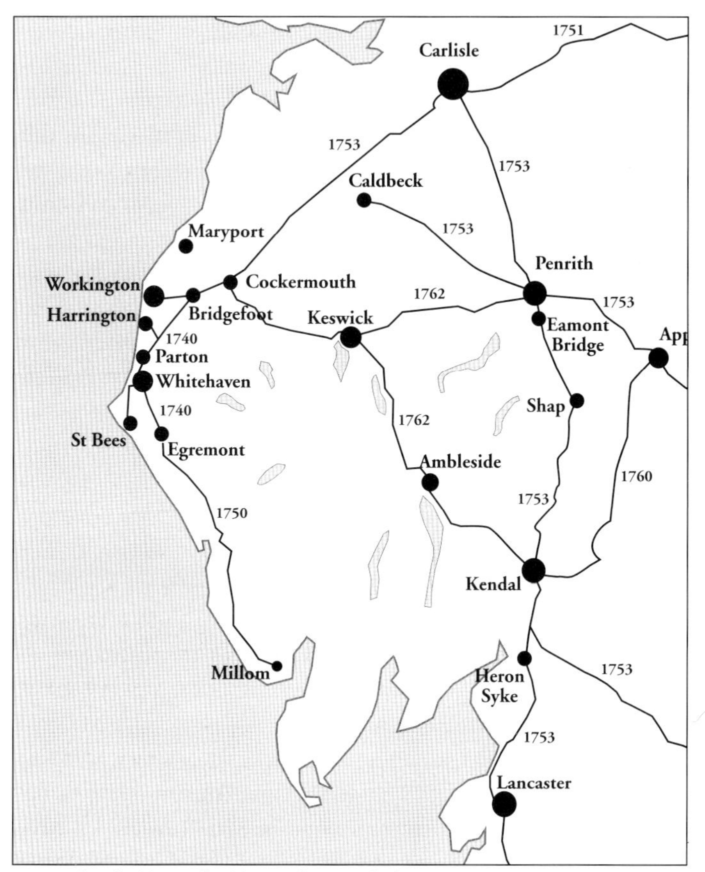

Map of early Turnpike Trusts in Cumbria.

coming from or going to over twenty different cities and towns. Just a few of these recorded teams in and out of Kendal were:

- To and from London, one gang every week of about twenty horses.
- From and returning to Wigan, one gang every week of about eighteen horses.
- From and returning to Penrith, two gangs every week of about fifteen horses each.
- From and returning to Whitehaven, one gang every week of about twenty horses.
- From and returning to York, one gang every week of about ten horses.

It was hard and a full day's journey, in the case of the Whitehaven gang, from the port to Kendal for it meant a crossing of the central

Lakeland Fells, via the notorious Hardnott and Wrynose passes. Even today by motor car this is no route for a motorist with weak nerves or doubtful brakes. Thus having made this arduous journey via pack horse, it is highly possible that the goods having been jogged continually, the tobacco had been reduced to dust and broken stalks and later purchased by Kendal traders at a nominal price, and this could have been how Kendal was introduced into the early snuff industry.

For this pack horse traffic and the succeeding wagon and coach traffic (this last increasing continually until the canal was brought into the town in 1819) Kendal provided over one hundred inns and overnight 'guest houses' with stabling accommodation, some of the larger inns and hotels catering for a hundred horses. One pack horse gang I did not mention above was the Glasgow one, this made the run regularly but at intervals longer than a week.

With all this varied commodity goods traffic meeting, off-loading and passing through, it is easy to see why Kendal became a town of many and varied trades, with its many water driven mills processing a wide variety of articles. For one thing these articles, if they were not manufactured from local materials, could easily be made from extraneous raw materials siphoned off from loads of such passing through the town. While all of these finished articles had to hand, a distribution system with access to a wide market, second to none in this horse transport age. An example of the way in which local products were traded for foreign raw materials is provided by the eighteenth century exchange of 'Kendal cottons' for raw, or leaf tobacco. This exchange occurred at the ports of Whitehaven and Liverpool, laden records kept at these ports bearing witness to these shipments; for Kendal's cloth went in exchange to the Americas. For the English town it was fortuitous exchange of resources, coming at a time when because living standards in Britain were rising, be it ever so slowly and slightly, and because of the competition from the expanding mills of Lancashire and Yorkshire, the home demand for Kendal's woollen cloths was declining. The blow to the Kendal industry was softened by this growing demand, Kendal cottons now finding a new and ready market in the southern states of America as clothing for the slave labour of the cotton and tobacco plantations.

The extent to which tobacco was indulged in at this period is a matter of history and song. Richard Braithwaite otherwise known as 'Drunken Barnaby,' wrote in the first half of the seventeenth century, speaks of great men's kitchens 'Where I suppose less smoke comes from their kitchen than their nose'. In an obscure mention of Kirkland, he deplores the existence of '...a kind of vermin who'd rather smoke a pipe than hear a sermon!' (J.F. Curwen)

So it can be seen that Kendal's love affair with tobacco in general and snuff in particular starting in a 'healthy' fashion early in the seventeenth century, continued to grow over the following years, nourished by a series of favourable factors of local and national, historical and environmental importance. Of course for the first hundred years or so the individual snuff manufacturers of Kendal were small concerns, situated in tobacco shops, or as was the custom then with regard to the sale of tobacco, in a wide variety of shops, and with the snuff being ground or powdered in hand operated mortars.

It is believed that the first water powered snuff mill was established in 1740 by Matthew Whittaker in a field to the right of the lane from Oxenholme Road to Kendal Parks a little over a mile south of Kendal. No traces of this mill remain today, though the location was known as Snuff Mill Meadow (or Close). Somervell quotes:

> 'The clearest indication is a large and deep depression in the field, which has undoubtedly been the mill pond, and some small traces of the mill above the stream, which is here carried underground. From the levels it would appear certain that the water wheel was 'undershot' moved by the stream running against it at its base. The stream is part of that which feeds the Natland Mill Beck mills pond, the portion flowing through Spindle Wood.'

Kendal Corporation showed keen business interest in the new industry. Placing an advertisement in the Newcastle Journal in 1755, it offered three snuff mills for rent at Castle Mills. A little later one of the by then three mills at Castle Mills, Kendal, was leased to a consortium of three local snuff manufacturers. Later still other neighbouring water mills were adapted for snuff grinding, and in the early years of the nineteenth century there was within a mile or so radius of the town a concentration of seven snuff mills.

The first Kendal tobacco 'magnate' or the first tobacco 'baron' of Kendal, was Thomas Tolson. He, in addition to preparing and blending tobacco on his own account, supplied most of the districts snuff manufacturers with raw tobacco leaf. By about the 1630s he had so far prospered that he was able to build Tolson Hall at Burneside, a few miles up the Kent from Kendal. Proud of his achievement and not ashamed of the sources of his wealth, Tolson incorporated into his mansion a pair of triangular stained glass windows displaying three tobacco pipes and two rolls of tobacco, carrying the following inscription:

> 'God by this means hath sent (1638) what I on this house hath spent. T.T.'

The other window showing three stacks of coins contains the caption:

> 'God by this means hath sent, what I on this house hath spent.
> All prayers be unto his name, that gave one meanes to build the same 1638'

However there is nothing in local records to substantiate this fact that he was merchant or manufacturer.

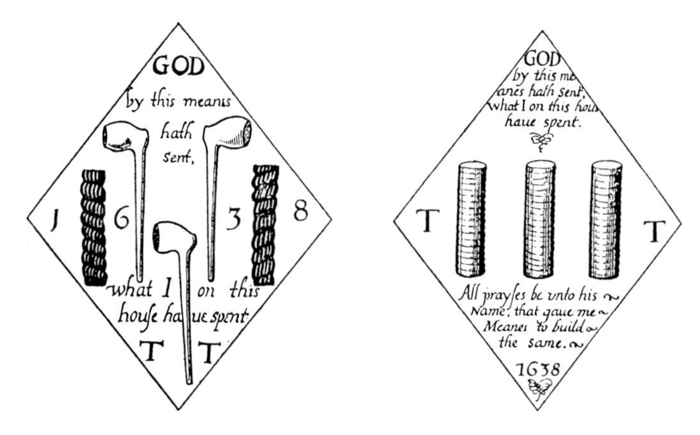

Picture of leaded windows at Tolson Hall

Nothing more is known of Thomas Tolson's connection with the tobacco business other than this memorial. Where he traded or manufactured is uncertain. It may have been Kendal, Bristol, London or even Virginia. One surmise is that he lived in Kendal and imported tobacco from Virginia in vessels that had taken out Kendal woollens to the planters. If however it was in Kendal it is remarkable that no local record is preserved.

It may also be added here, for the sake of interested readers who are not familiar with early snuff history, that the 'rolls of tobacco' in the window mentioned above, were *carottes*, the tight packed, six inch long, rolls of tobacco leaf from which hand ground or rather 'rubbed' snuff was made. (Supposedly named, in French, after the shape of that vegetable).

Old Kendal town directories and other significant documents of the time give the names of many small local snuff manufacturers operating during the nineteenth century. The little information known about these manufacturers is listed here.

Name	*Location*	*Years*
Matthew Whittaker [1]	Old Snuff Mill Oxenholme Rd	1740
	Fish Market	1805
James Simpson Jackson	Highgate	1828
Joseph Whittaker	Fish Market	1828–29
James Fothergill	Finkle Street	1828–34
Robinson & Allen [2]	Fish Market	1834–48
	New Road	1847
Mrs Ann Allen	Fish Market	1847–69
	New Road	1848
	Beezon Lane	1864–68
Peter Allen	Waterside	1873
Issac Farrer [3]	10 Finkle Street	1873–79
	Beezon Lane	1873–79
Mary Farrer	Sandes Avenue	1864
	10 Finkle Street	1885
Noble & Wilson [est 1852]	Market Place	1852–69
	Natland Beck Mill	1852–69
William Noble [4]	27 Market Place	1879–87
	56 Woolpack Yard	1879–87
	Natland Beck Mill	1879–87
James & Edward Busher [5]	Finkle Street	1858–79
	Highgate	1858–73
Graham & Dodgson	1 Mercers Lane	1869–73
	12 Market Place	1864
	Beck Mills	1865
David Parker [6]	Finkle Street/Collin Croft	1885–1925
Parker Brothers	Finkle Street/Collin Croft	1925

Notes
1 Knowledge gleaned elsewhere
2 Dissolution of partnership in 1848
3 Sold to David Parker December 1895
4 Taken over by Gawith & Hoggarth in 1887
5 1873 located in Berry's Yard
6 David Parker was Mary Farrer's manager

David Parker's premises in Finkle Street. *Margaret Duff Collection*

The carotte was held, or gripped, very tightly near to one end with the right hand, and this compressed end of the roll was rubbed up and down the tiny teeth of the 'rape' (or *rapée*), this last being French for a rasp. The rape (the apparatus was invented or developed in France in Nico's day, hence the names) was a kind of nutmeg grater, held in the left hand, and with a small, shallow box at one end in which to catch the snuff rubbed from the carotte; these portable 'do-it-yourself' snuff making machines were much favoured by the Continental and some British snuff users, and in course of time became highly ornamental. They gradually went out of fashion when machinery was invented to grind snuff more quickly and efficiently. The rasp in high circles had been an elaborate affair, with several appendages attached by fine gold or silver chains. These would include a small pin for freeing the grater's holes of snuff, a little rake to separate the rough snuff from the smooth, a spoon for transferring snuff from the rasp to the snuff box, and a hare's foot for brushing the snuff from the taker's upper lip. As you can imagine they are now much prized and collected.

Workmen in 1895 discovered many clay pipes during excavations for new buildings, which confirmed that pipe making was a subsidiary industry in Kendal.

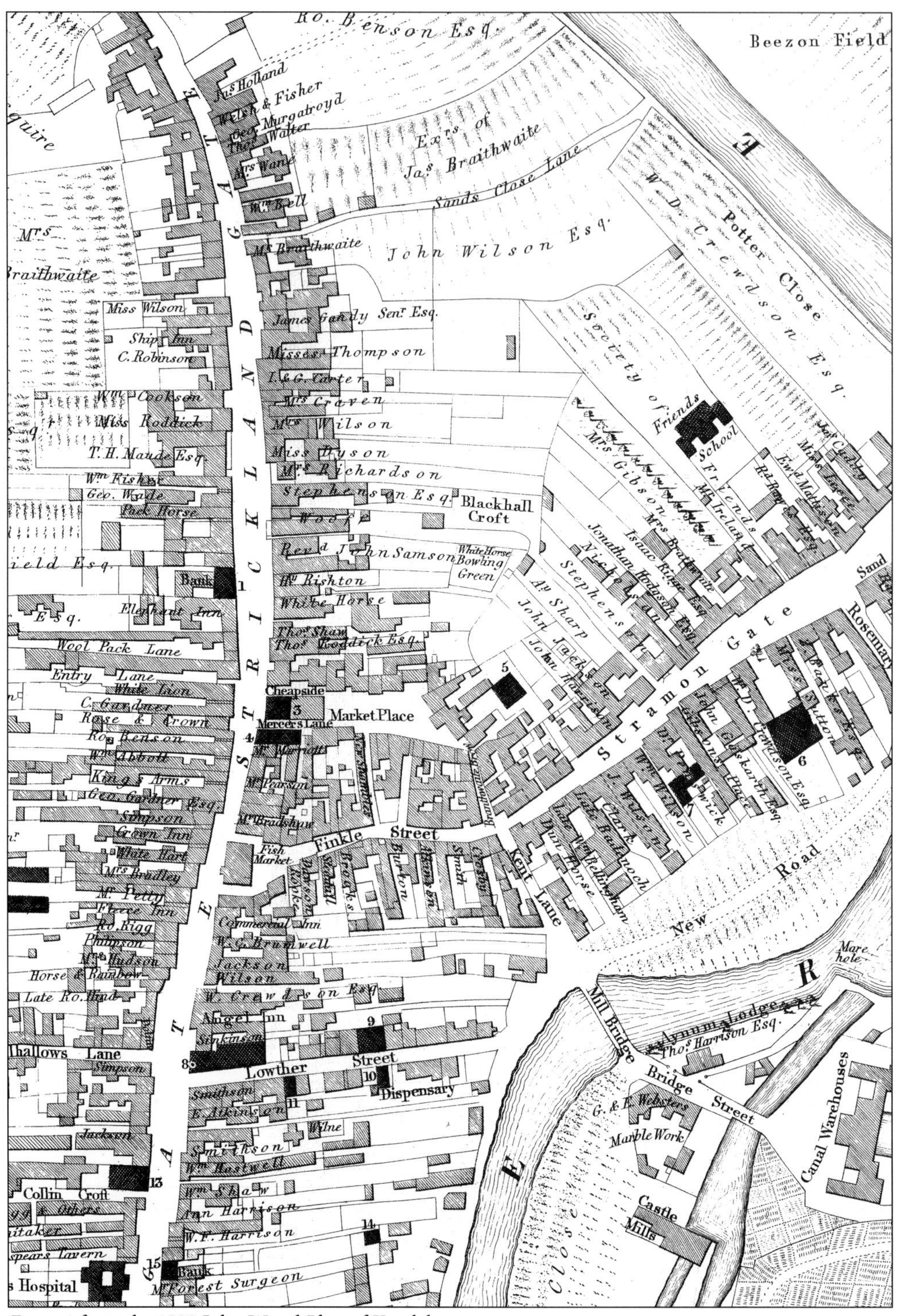

Excerpt from the 1833 John Wood Plan of Kendal

THREE

Samuel Gawith and Company

In the year in which george washington became the President of America and the French Revolution began, a Kendal man, moved no doubt by the rousing, independent spirit of the times, decided on a course of action as bold and daring as any of his more famous contemporaries. His name was Thomas Harrison and it is interesting to note that many of the Kendal snuff pioneers were called Thomas, though none of them were doubters! At this distance of just over two hundred years he remains a shadowy figure, but, although I have found no record of him earlier than this, it seems that he knew quite a bit about the tobacco and snuff business. It is also obvious, from later events, that he had an interest, probably recently acquired, in one of the Kendal district water mills.

Thomas Harrison's foray into Scotland

Having laid his plans and prepared the ground at Kendal, Harrison, in the following year, 1790, scraping together all his cash resources and bidding farewell to family and friends, took the plunge and set out for Scotland. His destination, in the first place, was Glasgow, then the recognised tobacco and snuff manufacturing centre of the whole of Northern Britain, if not of the whole of the British Isles. His aim was manifold, it was to acquire a knowledge of the technique of large scale, mechanized, snuff production (including how to operate and maintain the necessary plant and machinery), and then when he had acquired this operational 'know how', to purchase, new or second hand, as much of the requisite plant as he could.

Earliest Snuff Manufacturing Plant

Exactly how long Thomas was in Scotland in pursuance of these aims is not known. What we do know is that he more than fulfilled his expectations and his requirements. For in 1792, he returned to Kendal bringing with him a complete, though dismantled, snuff manufacturing plant of a considerable size, together with the skill and knowledge which would enable him to reassemble and operate it in its new home. This machinery, as it transpired, second hand, and then some fifty years old, was constructed, as the times dictated, in a very solid manner from oaken beams and huge, heavy cast and wrought iron gears, cog wheels and levers. The total estimated weight being some fifty tons.

It is easy in our day of heavy lorries and well made main roads, to overlook the stature of the transportation feat accomplished by Thomas Harrison, but with just a little imagination one can picture the train of groaning, heavily laden wagons, hauled by straining teams of horses, dragging its way over Shap Fell by the rough, unsurfaced, road of that time. A few years before such a feat would have been quite impossible. It is true that by 1792 the Turnpike Trust for the Kendal to Eamont Bridge, Penrith, stretch, had widened and to some extent levelled the way but it was not until 1826 that the road was surfaced by Kendal's then Borough Surveyor, the famous John Loudon Macadam, who, the very next year, was appointed Surveyor General of Metropolitan Roads. This in view of the great success of his surfacing system was first tried out on the Stricklandgate, Kendal, stretch of this same turnpike way in about 1824. This little piece of transport history usually forgotten today, but, without a surface and well drained one, this road between Penrith and Kendal could, in view of its locality, be nothing but rudimentary and dangerous. In fact it would be little better than it was in 1634 when the 'three travellers' went over it:

> 'through such ways as we hope wee neuer shall againe, being no other but climing and stony, nothing but bogs and myres, or the tops of those high hills, so as we were enforc'd to keepe these narrow, loose, stony, base wayes, though never so troublesome and dangerous…'
> (L.G. Wickham Legg, *A Relation of a Short Journey…* 1634 (London, 1904) pgs 41–42)

With the above in mind, however, it does give one some idea of what Harrison and his team accomplished if you stand, as I have done, and gaze at the main item of the load that was brought to Kendal in that year of 1792. This four mortar snuff mill or grinding machine by its size and solid construction and its great age, awakens a feeling of awe in the beholder, especially as one watches it still working perfectly and making snuff, after more than two hundred and fifty years of practically continuous use, but more about this now famous 'prize winning' machine later.(p68)

Reading an article in The Edgar Allen News (Vol 43 No 504) dated June 1964 – the author gives another easier solution that may have been used for the movement of the large cumbersome snuff mill – by sea from Glasgow to the old Westmorland seaport of Sandside, (now unnavigable), near Milnthorpe. From there it would be the matter of ten miles by road to Mealbank. Still a horrendous ten mile journey for the poor horses – but a far easier one. (There would still be the problem of loading and unloading, and crossing any bridges en-route.)

Mealbank Mill

So in spite of all obstacles, this first Thomas Harrison successfully transported his precious machinery from Scotland, proceeded to reassemble it and to install it in one of the three water driven mills at Mealbank, on the River Mint some two miles north east of Kendal. The cluster of water mills were situated inside the base of the first loop of an 'S' bend of the River Mint as it flows down from the slopes of Whinfell and lower Shap, on its way to the parent Kent. It is still today a very beautiful spot, with the made road ending in the yard common to all three of what were once the water mills. Up the slope to the right runs an unmade road leading up to Mealbank village, a quaint industrial hamlet of the former mill work-

Early photograph of Mealbank Mill showing workers cottages and manager's house behind the chimney and leading up the hill. *J Sawyers – John Marsh Collection*

ers' cottages, in scattered short rows. In the middle of one of these, that faces the mill buildings, is a much larger and quite imposing house and was the home of the manager of the mills, when they were all owned by one family or firm. He, of course, had to live on the site. The two smaller houses on either side would be occupied by the 'key-workers'. There was a small church (now a house) and a manse, and later a telephone box and a post box but no school or shop, and all the roads or ways are 'unadopted'.

Archaeologically the hamlet is worth a visit, but if you go to see the water mills you will be disappointed, they have disappeared under newer and less attractive buildings. It was a sunny afternoon when I visited the spot, and I talked with an old 'native' of the place who was sitting on a bench by his cottage door. He pointed out to me (in 1980) the site of the old 'snuff mill' and said that it had been pulled down forty odd years earlier. He also told me that when he was a boy, he and his friends would scrounge bits of tobacco leaf from the mill and go into hiding to smoke these pipes that they made from acorns.

Here it should be told that not only did Thomas Harrison bring back to Mealbank snuff machinery and 'know how' but also a snuff recipe or formula, and one for what was to become a highly popular and wide selling variety and brand of snuff. This was, and still is, the 'Original Kendal Brown', the 'original' being prefixed to the name in later years, when rival local snuff firms introduced their versions of 'Kendal Brown', for the product attained the same national fame in the nineteenth and twentieth centuries that 'Kendal Green' cloth enjoyed in the fourteenth and sixteenth. This 'original' (to 1792) snuff, of the dark, moist variety, is still today being made from this old formula which has been for the last two hundred or so years locked away in a bank strong room in Kendal, its secrets being known, and that by heart, to one or two only of the present firm's most trusted staff.

Brocklebank and Harrison – early beginnings

In, or soon after, 1792 Thomas Harrison lived in Highgate, Kendal, turning part of his premises into his town tobacco and snuff factory cum shop. There the snuff 'flour' was stored to mature, flavoured, packed and sold. Very early Harrison's 'flair' and the potential of his new venture was spotted by another keen businessman and neighbour in Highgate,

Left: The original mill that was brought down from Scotland in the background.

Thomas Brocklebank, 'chymist and druggist', as a Kendal Directory of 1805 puts it. He also, I believe, dealt, as many chemists did in that day, in tobacco and snuff. Brocklebank suggested to Harrison that they pooled their resources to develop the tobacco, and in particular, the snuff business, using the former's already well established shop as a prominent retail outlet. The proposal met with Harrison's approval, and the firm of Harrison and Brocklebank was born.

Lowther Street premises

It was about 1793, that another significant event in the life of Thomas Harrison took place. This was the birth that year of his son, also named Thomas. It was this Thomas Harrison, the second, who, after the death of his father, carried on the business with the ageing Thomas Brocklebank. It was also, I believe, this second Harrison who, around 1830, bought the premises at number 27, Lowther Street, for use both as residence and as a tobacco and snuff factory. That building has been from that day to this a centre of the same two trades. So it was at Lowther Street that Thomas Harrison's first child, a daughter Jane, born in 1819, grew from a child to become a young woman of some character, or, as the writer of an article on the history of the firm published in the trade journal 'Tobacco' in 1935, calls her 'a lovely, headstrong girl.' Being as she was, the granddaughter of the adventurous first Thomas Harrison, this description could well be a true one, though I rather think that the writer was largely basing his assessment on later events.

A recent picture of 27 Lowther Street, Kendal – nothing has changed.

*

Samuel Gawith the First

Samuel Gawith

Be that as it may, the young lady in question certainly proved irresistible to Samuel Gawith, a young man of Kendal, who, almost before he had attained his majority and completed his apprenticeship, fell madly in love with her. His courtship went very well, and he so won the affections of the young lady that before the end of 1837, with the girl barely eighteen years old, the couple had decided on an early marriage. The only trouble was that the girl's father did not share his daughter's feeling for Samuel, in fact just the opposite for he forbade them to meet never mind to marry. Matters reached a climax at the beginning of 1838 with the couple taking matters into their own hands by eloping to be married over the anvil at Gretna Green on the fifteenth of January 1838.

Time has made it difficult to trace much of Samuel Gawith's life prior to his marriage, but I believe, with good reason, that his father was also called Samuel, and that the son followed the father in his trade of plumber and glazier. Their family business, I believe, was situated in a Kendal 'Yard' on the east side of Highgate, just north of Cross View Yard, it would be No 107, or a yard very near to that number.

The bare announcement of Samuel's marriage in the Kendal Journals dated Saturday, 20 January, 1838, describe him as 'plumber and glazier of Kendal', and it is most likely, in view of her husbands youth, that it was at her father-in-law's house that the young bride passed the first years of her married life. However, in time father and daughter appear to have become reconciled in affection, for, when, in 1841, the former died, he left the premises at 27 Lowther Street and his share in the firm of Harrison and Brocklebank to his two daughters, Samuel's wife Jane, and her younger sister Ann. The will it appears containing a proviso that the young, unmarried girl was to have a home at Lowther Street under the care of her sister and brother-in-law.

In consequence of this Jane and her husband moved into Lowther Street to occupy the home there, with Samuel forsaking his old trade to, take up the place in the tobacco and snuff business vacated by the deceased.

Brocklebank & Gawith, Tobacco and Snuff Manufacturers

Whatever Harrison's feelings had been with regard to Samuel, his partner, Brocklebank seems to have had no reservations in accepting the entrance into the firm of his new partner, and the two appear to have got on well together. A Kendal Directory published soon after this gives 'Samuel Gawith, Snuff Manufacturer, H. (home) Lowther Street', and, in the 'Professions and Trades' section, 'Brocklebank and Gawith, Tobacco

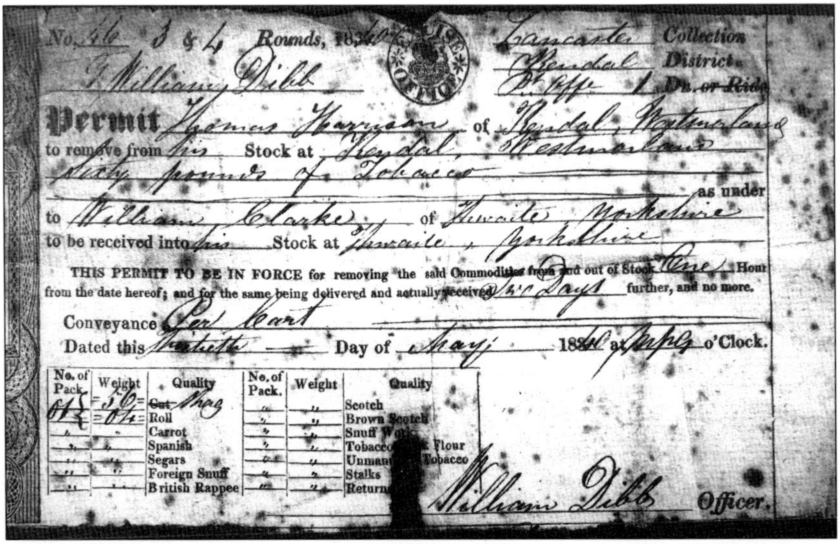

No. 46 3 & 4 Rounds, 1840 Lancaster Collection
William Dibb Kendal District

Permit Thomas Harrison of Kendal, Westmorland
to remove from his Stock at Kendal, Westmorland
Sixty pounds of Tobacco
as under
to William Clarke of Thwaite Yorkshire
to be received into his Stock at Thwaite, Yorkshire
THIS PERMIT TO BE IN FORCE for removing the said Commodities from and out of Stock One Hour from the date hereof; and for the same being delivered and actually received Two Days further, and no more.
Conveyance Per Cart
Dated this Twentieth Day of May 1840 at o'Clock.

No. of Pack.	Weight	Quality	No. of Pack.	Weight	Quality
		Cut			Scotch
		Roll			Brown Scotch
		Carrot			Snuff Work
		Spanish			Tobacco & Flour
		Segars			Unmanufactured Tobacco
		Foreign Snuff			Stalks
		British Rappee			Returns

William Dibb Officer.

Excise Permit of 1840 issued to Thomas Harrison (founder of company) by William Dibbs, (HM Customs). This was necessary so that manufactured tobacco could be moved from factory to trader.

and Snuff Manufacturers, Lowther Street and Finkle Street'. From which last it would seem that the retail shop had been moved from Highgate, this latter, Highgate, being now given as Brocklebank's home address.

Brocklebank's house and shop at Finkle Street, which formed part of the Brocklebank and Gawith premises, was sold off in 1847. When J.F. Curwen, in his book 'Kirkbie Kendal' mentions Waterloo House, Finkle Street, he states that the western portion was formerly occupied by James Fothergill, tobacconist, and then by Messrs Brocklebank and Gawith, also tobacco and snuff manufacturers.

The Gawiths were not in such a hurry to start a family, as they had been to marry, for it was not until November 1842 that their first child, a son, was born. He, like his father, was destined to play a major part in the unfolding story of this Kendal company, and he too was named Samuel. Over the next fourteen years five more children were to be born to the Gawiths, and of these five the first and the last, together with the eldest were to follow the father into the tobacco and snuff trade.

In December 1852 Ann Harrison died at Lowther Street, and the Harrison fortune passed, in its entirety, to Samuel Gawith and his wife. So, with the passing years, Samuel coincidently with the growth of his family, continued to grow in stature as a man of business.

On the death of Brocklebank, in the mid 1840s, he assumed sole control of the tobacco and snuff firm. In February 1852 a list issued by the Bank of Westmorland included, as one of the 'persons to whom the company or partnership belongs', the name Samuel Gawith, Kendal, Tobacco Manufacturer. And in spite of his ever-growing family and firm responsibilities Samuel entered fully into the civic life of Kendal.

In 1861 he was elected to serve as a councillor for the East Ward of the town. It says much for the quality of his service and of the esteem in which he was held that, after only four years in this last office, and at the comparatively young age of forty-eight, he was then elected Mayor, to become the leading citizen of his native town.

On the whole, however, the year 1864 was a sad one for Samuel Gawith, for on the 3 October his wife, Jane died. The father was left with a motherless family of six children, the eldest now twenty-one, the next a boy of seventeen and the youngest another boy of eight years. All these last mentioned three, were later to follow the father's example and become the heads of tobacco and snuff firms. Almost exactly a year after the death of his wife, on 9 October 1865, before finishing his year of office as Mayor, Samuel died. He was buried in the (then) new, small, cemetery at the head of Castle Street, joining there his wife. Later, in this same family grave were to be buried the couples' last two sons mentioned above, John Edward and William Henry. So that the one stone is memorial to the one time principles of no less than three independent tobacco and snuff firms, a unique albeit somewhat somber record.

Here, before moving on to the later history of the firm, we must pause and hark back a little and introduce into the story two persons, who though not connected with the Gawiths by family ties, had both already begun to play an increasingly important part in the lives and the drama of all three second generation snuff Gawiths and, in the case of one of the new entrants at least, in the story of Kendal's other and non Gawith snuff firm. First we must remember that at his death Samuel, whom we will now call Samuel Gawith the First, left a large orphaned family, and although it is true that the eldest son, Samuel Gawith the Second, had attained his majority, being at his father's death in fact twenty-two, and already a figure in the family business, he was still young to be head of a firm and a family (ranging in age from eighteen to nine years). So, wisely, Samuel the first, left his firm and his family in the hands of three trustees

Trustees

The first of these trustees was his elder son, Samuel the Second, of whom more later, but for now it is with the other two we are concerned. Here we should note that, by the very nature of their appointment, it is evident that Samuel the First had great respect for and confidence in, these two other, and older, men whom he chose to entrust so much to, just as it is also evident that his trust in the two was born of long and close acquaintance.

The first, and elder, of these other two trustees was Henry Hoggarth, a similar age to Samuel the First and his next door neighbour in Lowther Street and, I believe, a boyhood friend. When, in 1781–2, Lowther Street was laid out and built-up, number 29 was built as a family residence by a Captain Hoggarth (who was, I believe connected with a Kendal brewery firm), and the house is described in J.F. Curwen's 'Kirkbie Kendal' as 'The large house with the bold flight of stone steps at the south east corner' (of Lowther Street). The tall house, with its imposing flight of steps leading up to a wide front door, complete with iron foot scraper, is still there, and is still a fine building. Though, be it noted, it is no longer the last, or the corner house, as Curwen described it, for the well laid out garden that originally ran down from the house to the river and the end of 'Colonel's Walk has, this hundred years or more, been built over.

It was at this house in Lowther Street that Captain Hoggarth's grandson, Henry Hoggarth was born and grew up, and here that he became neighbour to his friend Samuel, when, in 1841, the latter moved with his wife to live and work at number 27. Unlike Samuel, Henry was not married then although with a business of his own. Henry Hoggarth was a land surveyor and the founder of a Kendal firm of land agents and surveyors, later estate agents with, finally, offices at Midland Bank Chambers, Highgate. The firm being carried on after Henry's death by his two elder sons. It is interesting to note that, in 1853, Henry produced his 'Lithographed Plan of Kendal.' He also became early in his professional career Superintendent of Lands to the Trustees of the Kendal Fell Lands that included Serpentine Woods, the Golf Course and Castle Howe. The 'Trustees being the mayor and elected councillors of Kendal.' Samuel the First was, from the time of his election as a councillor, one of these last, and this was just one of the many social and civic links which bound the two friends together. Ultimately two of Henry's children and one of Samuel's were to link the two families together with ties of business and even of marriage, but that is another and later chapter in the Kendal snuff saga, and mentioned here only in order to show that this 'Trustee' had a keen and lively interest in, and effect on the lives of those left in his charge.

The second of these non family trustees appointed by Samuel the first to watch over both his family and firm was the man who was to become the *raison d'etre* for the (chronologically speaking) second of the three Kendal snuff firms. He was in fact John Thomas Illingworth, who, at the time he was made a Trustee was, and had so been for some ten years, the commercial traveller, or representative ('rep' as we say today) for the Gawith firm. I believe that he had in fact been with the snuff and tobacco firm for most of his working life, and had now, by 1865, come to hold an important post in, and to be a valued servant of the company. But more about Illingworth in the chapter on his firm which follows this. It is sufficient to say here that the 'rep' was now some thirty-five years old, and that his 'boss' had, evidently, come to value Illingworth as man and friend as well as employee.

Samuel the Second and John Edward Gawith – 'Samuel and John E. Gawith, Tobacco and Snuff Manufacturers'

Following the death of their father, in 1865, the family business was taken over and run by the two elder sons, Samuel the Second and John Edward, as 'Samuel and John Edward Gawith, Tobacco and Snuff Manufacturers'. The business, including the snuff mill at Mealbank, having been left to the two brothers in equal shares. But, it should be noted, that the property at number 27 Lowther Street was bequeathed to the other children as a home for as long as they needed or required it; apparently with the proviso that the two elder brothers could have the use of the business part of the house on like terms. Samuel the Second, remember, being appointed one of the Trustees, and the family one, to ensure that these younger members of the family were kept and cared for until such time as they could fend for themselves.

With John Edward being only eighteen and a minor at law, a petition to the Lord Chancellor was necessary to enable him to take office as a director of the new company. This was formed under the direction and guidance of the two older Trustees, who, I believe, were also appointed to the board. The sanction to appoint John Edward having been obtained, the company under the management of the two brothers, continued to thrive and prosper during the decade following the death of Samuel the first. It must, however, have been a sad blow and something of a set back to the smooth running of the firm when, in 1867, John Thomas Illingworth left to found his own, and a rival company. But the company did survive, though no doubt it lost a number of its customers.

It was during this period, in the 1870s that the carved, life size figure of 'The Turk' was erected over the entrance to 27 Lowther Street. This original 'snuff shop sign' finally collapsed in 1973 and was replaced by a copy in 1975. I will mention these traditional snuff figures, and this one in particular in a later chapter (page 151).

For the first ten years or so of the partnership the two brothers apparently worked well together, but then differences between them grew and widened. Samuel had married a Scottish girl, while his brother's bride was Irish, and I have seen it suggested that a clash of national temperament in the two spouses was responsible for the friction between their husbands. However, from the knowledge that I have gathered of the two men, I rather think that the cause of the break lay in the characters of the men themselves, although it may have been fuelled by outside factors. That which drove them apart was not so much difference of character but sameness, for both were of a stiff, unyielding and military (I use the word advisedly) disposition. Both had a liking for, and even a gift of, command, for giving rather than for taking orders. In short they both wanted to be 'boss' and, I believe, that in the end the two agreed without bitterness to part company, in the duel sense, and be, each one, just that.

An Agreement of Separation

As a result, and once again with Henry Hoggarth acting as a wise counsellor and a just referee, in the year 1877, 'An agreement of separation' was drawn up, agreed to, and scheduled to come into force on 31 March 1878. From the nature and terms of this 'agreement', a photocopy of which I have before me as I write, I have concluded, as I hinted about, that this deed and act of separation was a 'gentleman's agreement', carried out with no ill will on either side.

The document in question is a most interesting one of three pages and ten clauses. The first clause is to the effect that from 31 March 1878 'the said partnership shall be dissolved', and that notice of the same 'be inserted in the London Gazette forthwith.' Clause three states that 'The shop and hereditaments situated in Lowther Street, Kendal ... shall be taken by one partner, and the snuff mill situated at Mealbank ... shall be taken by the other ... and that the said Samuel Gawith shall have his choice as to which of the two properties he will take.' Clause four sets out that the partner who takes the snuff mill shall have the snuff making machines housed at Lowther Street.

Henry Hoggarth's part in all this, as noted above, is attested to be clause six, which stipulates that 'Immediately after dissolution all books and papers ... shall be deposited at the office of Messrs Hoggarth Brothers, Land Surveyors, Kendal (Henry having by now turned his business over to his two elder sons, and the office being then at 69 Highgate) and shall be open at all times for the inspection of both partners.' Clause nine points out that the arrangements with regard to 27 Lowther Street is subject to the approval of 'the late Mr Samuel Gawith's Trustees and of the (other) children of the late Mrs Gawith, who are the owners of the property,' of whom some at least were, I believe, still living there. Clause ten reads 'Upon dissolution of the partnership ...either party shall be at liberty to manufacture tobacco and snuff, or tobacco, or snuff, at Kendal or elsewhere, and either party shall be at liberty to use such styles, terms, and trade marks, in reference to his future business as he lawfully can or may.' I have quoted this last clause in some detail because in one published account of the split it is stated that the agreement was that the brother who took the snuff side agreed not to manufacture tobacco, and the one who took the tobacco side agreed not to make snuff. The 'agreement', as quoted above makes it plain that no such restriction did in fact apply. In practice, however, the two brothers (or their two companies) did at first restrict themselves to the one chosen product. As a point of local interest the 'agreement was drawn up by Messrs Harrison and Son, Solicitors, Kendal'.

So it was that in 1878 two separate Gawith firms came into being, with the elder brother exercising his agreed right and taking, in the event, the snuff business with the mill at Mealbank, and, thereupon, styling himself Samuel Gawith, snuff manufacturer. This automatically left the younger brother, now thirty-one years old, with the tobacco side, which became John E. Gawith, tobacco manufacturer, Lowther Street.

Samuel must have found the old snuff mill at Mealbank small for the full carrying out of his business. The snuff business thrived and being a true son of his energetic father, Samuel, rather than seeking extra accommodation in some existing Kendal premises, set about planning and building a new purpose built factory.

Kendal Brown House

This factory complete with packing, sales and office facilities, was finished early in 1881, and was called, in honour of the firm's most famous brand of snuff, 'Kendal Brown House'. Very often this last, followed by Kendal, has served as the firm's postal address, although the full, present, address has Canal Head North, interspaced. The site of Kendal Brown House is at the old canal terminal adjoining the then, but now long since demolished coal wharves, and in an area once known as Great Aynham. Canal Head North forms a 'V'at its foot with a row of private houses called Little Aynam. Here Samuel the second bought a narrow strip of land stretching across the top of the 'V', building his works there.

John Edward Gawith

Meantime let us move backwards a little and take a look at the younger brother and his new firm. For a short while after 1878 John Edward Gawith ran the tobacco manufacturing business, concentrating mainly on making 'twist' tobaccos, but very quickly he decided to enter the highly lucrative snuff business. This was something that the terms of the division agreement allowed him to do, and which his knowledge of the manufacturing process fitted him to do, while his shared rights in the

Right: Aerial view taken in the 1930s showing Canal Head. The building centre right is Samuel Gawith's, with it's factory stretching back and chimney at the rear. The building stretching left is Illingworths Snuff & Tobacco. The canal head-race is shown to the left of the picture. *Aerofilms Ltd, Hendon / late Ken Edmondson*

Picture of Kendal Brown House 1940s

The Lowther-street Tobacco and Snuff Manufactory, Kendal.

ESTABLISHED 1792.

In consequence of the Government having increased the duty on Tobacco, my price for **Gawith's Kendal Brown Snuff** will in future be —

Loose in Cask or Bladder ... 3/11 per lb.
In 1, 2, 4, or 6lb. tins......... 4/1 ,,

I shall shortly send you framed Show Card, and trust to be favoured with your orders.

Faithfully yours,

JOHN E. GAWITH.

A card giving the price of Kendal Brown Snuff sold loose in cask or bladder, showing proprietor as John E. Gawith.

Gawith recipes and trademarks was an added incentive. At first to carry out this purpose John may have installed a small snuff grinding mill at Lowther Street, but soon he acquired a larger, water-driven grinding plant at Low Mills, just south of Kendal, in what had previously been an iron foundry. So with this rapid expansion the new firm seemed all set to prosper.

However John Edward does not seem to have had the business acumen and judgement of his father and elder brother, and expanding too fast, overstretched his financial resources and became bankrupt after a run of seven years. In discharge of this bankruptcy John Edward's goodwill, trademarks, and recipes for snuff, were sold and bought back by his brother Samuel. Thus the famous 'Original Kendal Brown', and other formulas together with the 'dog' trade mark etc became once more the sole rights and property of one firm. We do not know much else about John E. Gawith except that he died after another seven years, in 1892.

Samuel Gawith the Second

We can now return to the main stream of our story and to Samuel Gawith the Second. One immediate effect of the 1885 takeover by him of the goodwill etc of the defunct tobacco firm was his determination to carry on making and supplying the tobacco products latterly produced by the bankrupt concern. He strongly desired to retain this custom and trade which his brother, and before him, his father, had built up. Accordingly Samuel applied for and received from the Inland Revenue, on the 6 July, 1885, a license to manufacture tobaccos at all his Kendal premises.

With regard to Samuel the Second's Kendal premises it seems that following the failure of his brother's firm, the elder brother used 27 Lowther Street for the next two years; for Bulmer's Westmorland County Directory published in the latter half of 1885, gives the business address of Samuel Gawith Tobacco and Snuff Manufacturer as 'Great Aynham and Lowther Street' (we shall see later why he did not use 27 Lowther Street for more than two years). This same 1885 Directory also gives us Samuel's private address as Greenbank, which I take it to be the house in Horncop Lane, Kendal. Samuel the Second was, of course, now a married man living within a mile of his new works, with his Scottish wife. The lady's maiden name being, Anderson, something of which she was very proud. The couple were blessed with five children, four daughters and one son. Charlotte Emily was born in 1874, and lived, unmarried, until 1941, but

General Licence.—No. 344—1.

No. 736 No. K1R 2

Carlisle Collection.

I, the undersigned, duly authorized by the Commissioners of Inland Revenue, hereby grant Licence to Samuel Gawith & Co residing at Little Aynam in the Parish of Kendal and County of Westmorland to exercise and carry on the under-mentioned Trades at the Premises aforesaid, but nowhere else, from the day of the date hereof, until and including the Fifth day of July next ensuing, he having paid for this Licence the undermentioned Duties chargeable by Law in respect of the several Licences to exercise the said Trades, and amounting altogether to the sum of £0 · 5 · 3

Dated this sixth day of July 1885

	£	s.	d.
Tobacco Dr	—	5	3
Total......£	—	5	3

Gmarkesh

Collector of Inland Revenue.

INLAND REVENUE OFFICE

[861] 4,200 bks 10/83

Licence from the Inland Revenue dated 6 July 1884 to Samuel the Second

Evelyn Anderson Gawith, born in 1881 lived only three years, having died in 1884. The parents had to wait until this last year, 1884 for the birth of their only son, Samuel Anderson Gawith, who will, later, fill his role in our story of Samuel the Third.

Albert Philipson and John Rigg – Mealbank

In this same year of 1885 a boy called Albert Philipson started work at the Mealbank Mill, joining there, and commencing to learn the trade of snuff grinding, under John Rigg. Rigg had then been with the firm some seven years, and was soon to become snuff grinding foreman in succession to his father, having served his time and learned the trade under him. Both these men remained with Gawiths for the rest of their working lives, Mr John Rigg for almost sixty years, becoming the snuff manager of the firm, and, I believe, during his last years a director; while Mr Philipson followed Mr Rigg as snuff foreman.

It will be noted from the foregoing, that on his brother's bankruptcy Samuel the Second did not take over the snuff milling plant at Low Mills (he probably did not need it), nor did he acquire permanently the plant and premises at 27 Lowther Street. I stress here this last point because it will have an important bearing on the events of the year 1887, soon to follow. But, before this, we have 1886, the year in which, on 27 November, at the comparatively young age of forty-four, Samuel Gawith the Second died.

Samuel Gawith the Second – the man

What kind of a man was Samuel the Second, apart that is, from his undoubted business success in establishing the new factory, Kendal Brown House, and uniting the once divided firm? Unlike his father he was not a great figure in the civic life of Kendal, although he did serve one year as a member of the town council, 1870–1, but in another sphere he rose to the very top of local fame. So much so that at his death the flag of the Town Hall 'was hoisted at half mast, a token of public sympathy and respect' (to quote a local newspaper). For Samuel was a soldier, a pillar of the pre-Territorial Forces, the 'Voluntary Army', or 'Volunteers'. He joined the 'Westmorland Volunteer Rifles' on their formation in 1859, at the age of seventeen, as a private and was sworn in on the 11 January 1860. He then went on to hold every post in the ranks, including twenty-three years as an officer, being commissioned as an ensign on the

Samuel Gawith the Second

10 November 1863, as soon as he reached his majority. This commission, granted and signed by the Corps Colonel-in-Chief, Lord Lowther, may be seen in the Archives at County Hall, Kendal.

Samuel was promoted Captain in 1873, Major in 1878, and raised to the honorary rank of Lieutenant Colonel, 'for long service', on 12 June 1886. Not bad for a 'little chap' who, because of the shortness of his legs, had difficulty in keeping his seat when his mount moved at more than walking pace. It was written of him on his death that he was 'Captain of the Old X Company. An able and zealous officer, a strict disciplinarian, but popular with his men. A supporter of shooting, giving a cup to be competed for! He was the main force in getting Kendal Drill Hall, in Queen Katherine Street built, and lived to see it almost completed.' In view of this it is hardly surprising that he was given a military funeral, and one of the biggest ever seen in Kendal. 'There was a muster of some two hundred men of the 'Volunteers' under Captain Gillow, and with fourteen other officers present. While from the Town Hall to St. Thomas's Church the cortége was headed by a military band which played the 'Dead March' from Handel's oratorio 'Saul'. We are told, in the same local newspaper's account of the funeral quoted above, that the mourners in the first carriage included 'Major Gawith, Master Gawith, Dr Jackson Gawith, Mr Harrison Gawith and Mr W. H. Gawith.' Of these Gawiths I presume that the first mentioned, the Major, was John Edward, Master was Samuel's infant son, and the last was the deceased's youngest brother, William Henry.

So Samuel Gawith the Second died and was buried in the family grave on the south side of St. Thomas's Church, Kendal. Reintered with him was his infant daughter, Evelyn Anderson, who had died less than two years before. Then later his wife, his elder daughter, Charolotte Emily, and finally his only son, Samuel Anderson, would join him.

Before moving on to continue the later pages of the Samuel Gawith and Company story let us pause and look briefly at the first, and at the last, of the Gawiths mentioned above as filling the funeral coach. The first, John Edward died in 1892, surviving his brother by six years and dying like him at the age of forty-four. The second of these two, William Henry, the youngest of Samuel the Second's brothers, we may introduce here as shortly to be, in the very next year, 1887, one of the founders of the third of the three inter-related, present day Kendal snuff firms. He is a character of whom I will say more in the later chapter on him and his firm.

Samuel Gawith the Third

Samuel the Third, or Samuel Anderson Gawith, was a child of two years and five months at the death of his father, and so once again the family business was left in the hands of trustees. Three of these, I believe were the mother of young Samuel Anderson, and his two uncles mentioned last above. However from what I have just written about these last two it will be realized that their influence on the life of the firm was comparatively short lived and (or) quickly diminished, the one dying after a few years and the other, William Henry, naturally being occupied with his own firm and its affairs. The continued growth and success of Samuel Gawith and Company under these circumstances then, is I think, a great

Samuel Gawith the Third

tribute to the staff and work people of the firm at this time. It speaks volumes for the devotion and ability of company servants such as John Rigg and Albert Philipson, who would be mainly responsible for the snuff production during this period.

It should be remembered that this transitional period between the death of Samuel the Second in 1886 and the coming of age in 1905 of Samuel the Third (and of his consequential taking over of the reins) was a crucial one in the history of the firm, which would be much affected by the stirring events of the time. To mention only three of these events, the Boar War; the change in the Monarchy, and the coming of the motor car. Incidently it was one of the men mentioned above, Albert Philipson, who after fifty years with the firm, and in an interview for a magazine article, in 1935, recorded his boyhood memories of the militant Samuel the Second, in words to the effect that, 'Sam was a little stiff chap, who was always riding round the streets of the town on his white horse, although he just wasn't built for riding, and, it's a good job he wasn't alive when the Boar War came, for he'd have had us all enrolled in the army and off to South Africa!'

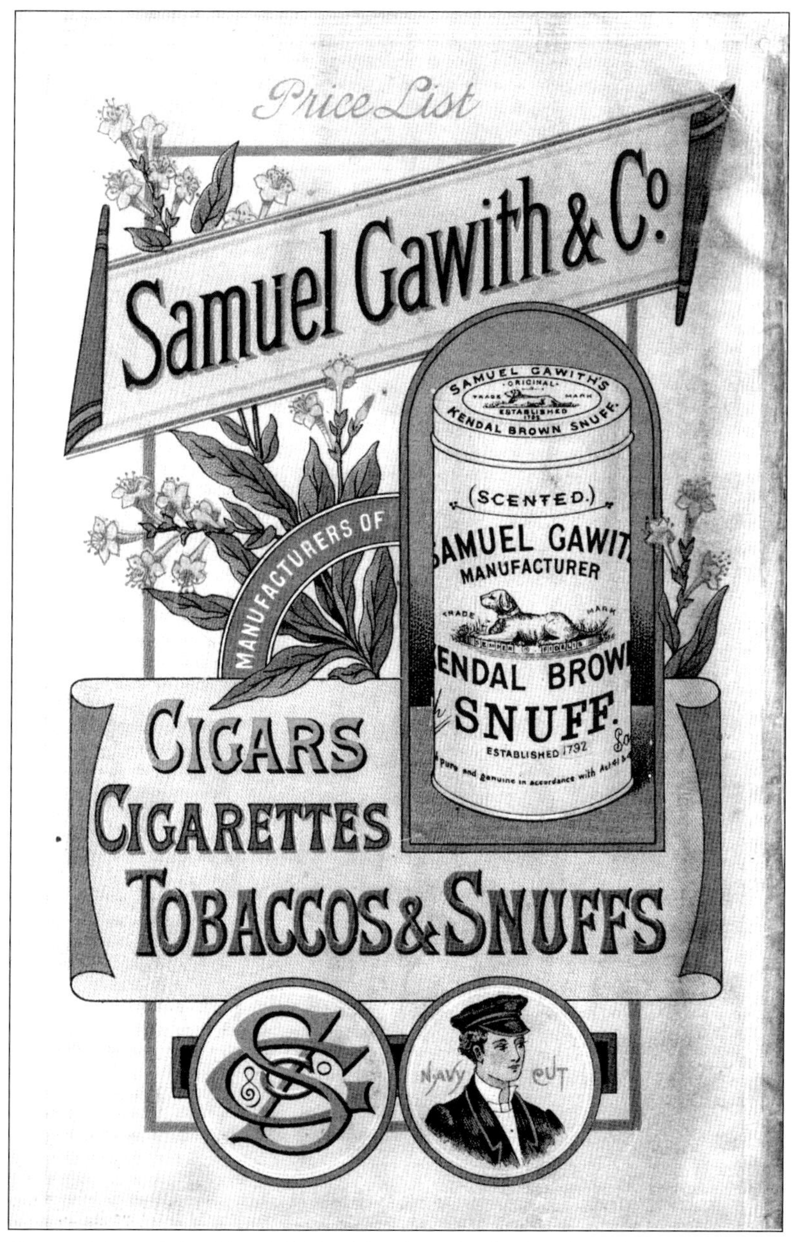

Cover of Samuel Gawith 1900 Price List. Note the dog 'trade mark'

Kendal Record Office

Mr W. Pennington

Another figure that undoubtedly played a great part in the company's survival over this period and up to 1920 was Mr W. Pennington. He succeeded J.T. Illingworth as commercial traveller for the firm, and rivalled this last in the quality and length of his service. Mr Pennington for forty eight years represented 'Gawiths' on the road, travelling in that time all over what is now Cumbria, and in addition much of Lancashire, the West Riding of Yorkshire and South West Scotland. All this in pre-motor car days (or at least pre for 'reps'), in fact he always used a pony and trap and with these was a familiar sight in the Lake District, until he retired around 1920. His job was not to deliver orders, this could be done by lesser men and by rail where possible, but to win the orders and even more importantly, to collect the cash. Sometimes he would return from a lengthy trip laden with golden sovereigns and guineas, and at other times he would have to find room in his trap for ten pounds worth or more of pennies (with 240 to the pound remember!). It is said that he carried, and let everyone know that he carried, a revolver, 'a heavy cumbersome affair that never all the time that Mr Pennington had it shot anything more dangerous than a rabbit!' Samuel thought well of him with the proviso 'that he always insisted that he set off and returned to the factory.'

So we arrive at the twentieth century, with from around 1904–5 the firm under the control of Samuel Anderson Gawith, or Samuel the Third. This is neither the time nor place to dwell on the many varieties of snuff or the production, but one story that is told of the early years of this century and of Samuel the Third's reign, concerns the oils and essences added to produce the wide range of long popular 'scented' snuffs. These distilled and concentrated essences such as Bergamotte, lavender, sandalwood, carnation and attar of roses are very expensive, especially this last; and it seems that Samuel Gawith & Co. had in 1908, bought and paid for a large quantity of these oils from the producers in Scicily. The consignment was stacked on the quay at Messina awaiting shipment to England when the great earthquake of that year occurred and the whole of the precious load was destroyed. The whole city was destroyed with a loss of life given at 96,000 souls, a total only once exceeded in recorded history. It appears that the consignment was not insured, or at least not against loss by earthquake, and its loss was a great financial blow to the Kendal company. As a result it is said that the staff were made to work much longer hours for no extra pay in order to offset the loss and keep the firm going.

Above and overleaf: Advertising posters for Samuel Gawith & Co.

SAMUEL
GAWITH

AND CO'S

FOR DISCRIMINATING SMOKERS
WHO WANT QUALITY

1oz. Packet 1/-

SAMUEL GAWITH & Co. LTD.
The original Kendal Brown Factory
KENDAL

The Workers

Wages were low and girls were paid 4s. (20p) a week and in 1900 this rose to 6s. (30p) a week. The men, if they were very good at their jobs, received 30s. (£1.50) a week. For overtime the hands were paid 1s. (5p) for nine hours.

Those were times when the pubs opened at six in the morning, and when workmen sometimes appeared the worse for wear and snuff workers were once discovered having smuggled a five-gallon cask of ale into the factory.

Transport

The problem of transport in those alleged 'good old days' must have been great. True the railway had come to Kendal, but the railway was not always convenient for outlying districts. We also had our canal that was on the doorstep. By road it was by horse and cart, or, in bad weather, by packhorse.

Bladders used for storing snuff

An item of interest was that at one time snuff was sold packed in cows' or pigs' bladders. They kept the snuff in good condition and they would hold anything from 10-20 lbs and were cheaply obtained from the local slaughterhouse. Hooks which they supposedly hung off are still in the ceiling in Samuel Gawiths today. They are similar to what you used to see the hams hanging off in farmhouses. For larger quantities casks were made using wood from the hogshead that came from the American packers. Nothing was wasted.

Westmorland Gazette – 14 March 1903

On 14 March 1903 the Westmorland Gazette carried an article describing how the various kinds of tobacco were processed.

> Two casks; the one is known as a tierce of Virginia tobacco leaf and contains eight or ten cwt. The other is a hogshead of Kentucky leaf and holds perhaps twelve or fourteen cwt. Half-a-dozen other different growths are lying in stock, some destined for tobacco, some for cigars, some for cigarettes – leaves from Syria, Japan, China, Borneo, Cuba, Java – Latakia for mixtures; light Virginia for flakes and cigarettes; dark

Virginia and Kentucky for twist; Chinese and Japanese for cut tobacco and blending; rich bales from Cuba, Java, Sumatra for cigars. Let us turn to our casks of Virginia and Kentucky. These are the staple on which the manufacture is based. The leaves are so rammed and jammed together that you would think it impossible to disentangle them. But to separate them is a necessary step to the part they have afterwards to play. Therefore they are taken forthwith to a steamer, a large open trough with a canvas bottom, through which the steam penetrates the whole mass, without adding much to its moisture, and so makes it possible to take leaf from leaf without tearing them. The next remove is to the 'liquoring vat.' Into this the leaf is weighed in portions of 100 lb, and water is sprinkled over it in carefully measured quantities. (The watering is a delicate operation, about which something more must be said presently). Now the leaf is ready for spinning, a vital business with Kendal tobacco operatives.

The object is to turn out those rolls of *twist* – light brown, dark brown and black – which form a familiar yet puzzling feature of the tobacconist's stock. The spinning is done on some machines by hand, on others be steam. The tobacco spinning rather resembles rope-spinning but whereas a rope is spun in the air tobacco is spun on a table. At the one end of the table is the spinning wheel; at the other are women laying out the leaves ready for the spinner. He takes them, begins at the wheel, forms a core of twist with the smaller leaves, saves the large ones for the outer covering, and as the wheel keeps the whole constantly turning, the spinner adds as constantly to its length, until the other end of the table is reached. The line of twist is then wound up into a coil, and the process is repeated day in day out. The spinner learns by experience exactly what thickness to make his twist so that a given number of inches of any size will weigh a pound. The operation just described is that of spinning by hand.

The *steam spinning machine* operates much more rapidly and simply. The spinner, instead of walking away from the wheel and forming the twist as he goes, stands close to it, keeps up a supply of leaf, and regulates the size of the twist; the machine does the rest. There is a fine pigtail, a thick pigtail, a bogie, and two sizes of Irish. The care and labour lavished on the production of the black twist is astounding. It gets a dressing of olive oil, which is denied to any other, and when it has been wound into rolls either large or small, it is put into a steam press for a day. Thence it emerges very much compressed, but very tender. A cold press for a week is its next experience; and when released from that it would give many points in toughness to the toughest Wensleydale cheese. Its supreme merit is that 'it takes some chigging.' The darkest leaf that ever grew in Virginia or Kentucky would not recognise itself in its changed condition.

So much for the pigtail and twist. The treatment of flake is simpler. The leaf is packed in strong wooden moulds of varying width and depth, and subjected to great pressure under blocks fitting into the moulds, and operated by a screw press. Thus a mould eight inches deep is filled with leaf, laid in smoothly and evenly. Under pressure it is consolidated into a 'stick' only two inches deep. Without more ado it is ready for the steam cutter which acts like a guillotine, and cuts cake tobacco more easily than *mater familias* cuts bread. The cake or 'stick' of tobacco as it is called in the factory, keeps its shape under the cutter, being merely divided into thin slices from one end to the other. All that remains is to distribute it into the packets or boxes in which it is sold, and the factory has done with it.

For *shag* tobaccos and mixtures another set of operations is adopted. The leaf goes in its loose state to a different kind of cutting engine, driven by steam, and capable of dealing with 100 lb in twenty minutes. It is cut into a fine or a coarse strand at the will of the operator, and when it leaves the machine it has been changed from leaf into tobacco which he who runs may recognise. If it is to form part of a mixture it goes to a machine like a *chevaux de fries* shut up in a cylinder. The *chevaux de fries* revolves and the mixing is a matter of course. These tobaccos are also stoved, a ceremony which consists in spreading a mass out on an open slab, which is heated from below, while a workman turns and draws the tobacco with as much apparent affection as a woman displays in kneading her dough. He seems loth to leave it, but at last he is prevailed upon to spread it out on frames to cool; and so it too is ready for the packing room.

It would be hazardous to say in how many different forms Kendal tobacco is 'put up' for the market. There are thirty or forty names for it, with registered marks, special packets, boxes and wrappers. The selection of these is not the part of the business in which the least ingenuity is manifested; for nowadays it does not matter what the manufacturer or the merchant has to sell, he tries to catch the eye and ear of his customer as the best way of approaching his senses as a whole, and his pocket in particular.

Cigar making is a comparatively recent innovation in Kendal. Side by side with it is carried on the manufacture of the democratic cigarette. Both operations are performed by hand. There are good judges who consider that a hand-made cigar is a more comfortable 'weed', to smoke than the machine-made article, because it draws more freely. Experts may settle the point for themselves. The building of a cigar is a very simply process; yet as every social being knows to his sorrow it is possible to do it very badly. There are jerry-built cigars, as there are jerry built houses. In Kendal, of course, there is no jerry-building of either kind. There are three qualities of leaf in a cigar: (1) the 'filler', which is the core of the cigar; (2) the 'bunch', in which the core is secured; (3) the 'wrapper' which envelopes all.

A woman sits at a bench with a supply of the necessary materials before her; and almost as quickly as one can describe it, filler, bunch and wrapper pass through her fingers, the cigar is rolled and shaped, the wrapper gummed and cut, and she is repeating the same set of movements on another cigar. To the eye of the novice one cigar in the finished pile looks exactly like another. The adept, however, perceives that they are of different shades of the same colour; for the simple reason that there are different shades of brown in different leaves on the same tobacco plant. Therefore they have to be sorted so that the contents of each box shall be as nearly as possible of the same shade. And having been labelled and boxed they are despatched to the drying room, an apartment kept at a temperature of about 90 degrees. So you see the proper curing of the dead tobacco leaf needs a greater heart than that which induces the seed of the living plant to germinate. Cigars vary, as every schoolboy knows, in shape, size and weight. But even the schoolboy does not always know how difference of quality is produced, because he does not know how many kinds of Cuban tobacco leaf there are, nor how they are blended to form the 'filler', nor where the best 'wrappers' come from, nor precisely how much pressure is needed to give cohesion and unity of effect to the whole. This is the art of the professional cigar maker; and as practised in Kendal the schoolboy no doubt would find it a fascinating art too. As to the rolling of a cigarette the amateur would not have much to learn from the professional, except in point of facility.

Not too much water, but just water enough.

This is the ideal of the tobacco manufacturer of today. It has been told how at a certain stage of preparation the leaf is put into a liquoring vat and watered. Until about two and twenty years ago there was no legal limit to the water that might be added. Then it was fixed at 35 percent as a maximum. Now it is 30 percent, and bad luck to the maker who is caught treating his customers to an excess. Now the leaf as it arrives in this country holds about 14 percent of water. One of the first duties of the manufacture is to ascertain by testing how far his actual samples are above or below this average. According to the result of the test so is the added water regulated. On a hundred pounds of leaf he may pour twenty to twenty-five pounds of water. There will then probably be a total of rather more than the legitimate 30 percent, but in the process of manufacture some moisture will evaporate, and the finished tobacco will come out with a maximum moisture of about 28 percent. 28 percent is unvexed security; 29 percent perfect bliss; 31 percent apprehension. For a tobacco factory is always open to the inspection of the officers of the

Inland Revenue, who not only collect the duty before the manufacturer gets his raw material, but take an official interest in the quality of the finished product. Last year the total weight of the tobacco cleared for duty in Kendal was upwards of 160 tons, and the duty at 3s. (15p) per lb exceeded £54,000. On an average, thereon, the Kendal manufacturers between them pay £1,000 a week in duty all the year round.

Sandes Avenue Factory – 1920 'The Tobacco Factory, Kendal'

And keep going the firm did, right through the First World War of 1914-18, when, owing to the disruption of production in other centres, tobacco, and particularly snuff production at Kendal was stepped up to meet a growing demand. By the end of hostilities in late 1918 Samuel Gawith Co. was ready to expand. A plot of land was acquired at the Stricklandgate end of Sandes Avenue, Kendal. On this plot, just down from the corner, and adjoining Illingworth's Works, a purpose built factory was erected and opened in 1920. Into these new premises was transferred the old snuff making plant which for a hundred and thirty years had been making snuff at the water mill at Mealbank. This meant that the plant, some of it fifty years old when it was installed at Mealbank in 1792,

Above: The Snuff Factory, Sandes Avenue.

began yet another lease of life in another setting, but this time driven not by water but by electricity.

It was planned to erect, later, on the Stricklandgate/Sandes Avenue corner site a large sales shop and office block as an addition to the factory. This extension was never built but the plans for it are preserved in the Archives Department at County Hall, Kendal. Some of the firms tobacco production was, I believe, also transferred to the new Sandes Avenue premises, which was known by the name of 'The Tobacco Factory, Kendal.' The firms other premises, Kendal Brown House at Canal Head, meanwhile continued to house the company offices, packaging department and much of the finishing plant for both snuff and tobacco.

Takeover of Messrs William Nevinson's, Eamont Bridge

The next, the final to date, expansion of the firm took place in the early 1930s, when Samuel Gawith & Co. took over the Penrith Tobacco and Snuff Manufacturing firm of Messrs William Nevinson. This old established firm had their snuff grinding plant housed in an ancient water mill at Eamont Bridge, just outside Penrith. The mill was situated on the River Eamont, which flows out of Ullswater, passing just south of Penrith on its way to join the Eden.

It had been first a corn mill, then a gunpowder mill and since 1835, a snuff mill, and it contained among its machinery a unique milling machine named Edgerunner, that I will mention again later when it took on the name of Jumbo!

Gawiths disposed of the Penrith firm's tobacco business and premises but kept the snuff mill, putting in some new plant in 1934 to supplement the old. This was a very busy time for the company, and especially for their snuff manager, Mr Rigg, now seventy-two years old. At this advanced age he assumed responsibility for snuff production at both the Kendal works and at the Eamont Bridge Mill, travelling between the two, on an average twice a week, by motorcycle. Not bad going as this meant negotiating Shap Fell in winter as well as summer.

Snuff production only – Kendal Brown House

This decade of expansion in the company and its affairs called for a cash input and a wider based management. Accordingly in 1929, Mr Derek

Left: John Rigg at the High Snuff Mill, Eamont Bridge, near Penrith, and the workers looking out of the windows.

Snuff being sifted at Eamont Bridge.

Edgerunner – old rolling grinder, at Eamont Bridge Mill, this was later transferred to Kendal and is still working today – 'Jumbo'. *Atkinson & Pollitt, Kendal*

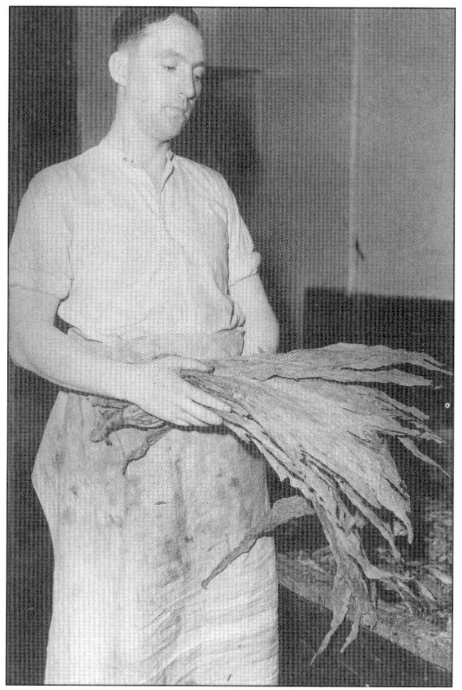

Tobacco leaf tester/liquorer holding A few 'hands' of tobacco – used in the manufacture of certain types of snuff.

John Rigg aged 72 years old used to travel between Eamont Bridge Mill and Kendal on his motor cycle once a week over Shap. His recipe for health – 'Plenty of Westmorland air and Kendal snuff!'

Dakeyne-Cannon became a shareholder in the firm and at the same time was appointed managing director, Mr Gawith becoming chairman of the board of management. The mid and late 1930s was a time of fierce competition in the tobacco and cigarette trade and saw many mergers and takeovers, particularly of the smaller firms. One feature these smaller companies found hard to combat was the expansion of the gift coupon schemes, run by so many of the major tobacco and cigarette companies, which caused a big swing in public demand to their products. In the case of Samuel Gawith & Co. the result of this tougher climate was a decision in 1936 to concentrate all production on snuff, and in fact all the activities of the firm, under one roof. To implement this decision work was started on extending the Kendal Brown House premises at Canal Head by the building on to them of a machine shop, and one large enough to accommodate both the Sandes Avenue and the Eamont Bridge plant.

Eamont Bridge Mill closure – 1937

So 1937 saw the closure of one more of Cumbria's old water mills, the one at Eamont Bridge, and the vacation by Gawith's of the Sandes Avenue premises. Also, and amazingly, the old snuff grinding machine, bought second hand and brought to Kendal in 1792, was yet once more dismantled and then reassembled in yet another new home, to begin anew working faultlessly and producing still more snuff. Today, another two hundred and eleven years on from then, it is still doing the same, a triumph of British workmanship, and a great tribute to the quality and skill of its Scottish builders of some two hundred and fifty years ago.

Picture Cards

It was I believe, about this time when all production of cigarettes was stopped, but, owing to a great extent to the world wide fame of and demand for the firm's snuffs and in particular the 'Kendal Brown' range, the tobacco side was able to continue unchecked, and, in the late 1930s a healthy export trade with the USA was established. Two of the firm's tobaccos that were popular in America were 'Grouse Moor Rubbed Flake' and 'Skiff Mixture,' this last being packed in vacuum tins. It was with these two brands, and for the American market, that the firm issued in 1939 its one and only set of picture cards. This was entitled 'The English Lakeland' and was a series of black and white photographic studies of Lakes views, measuring 3½" × 2¾". These cards are now extremely rare, and hard to collect in good condition, as only a mere six hundred sets, with twenty-five cards to the set, were issued, and most of these went to the USA. The text on the reverse of the cards ends 'The House of Samuel Gawith, Kendal. Est. 1792. Presented in each vacuum tin of Fine Tobacco. Manufactured in the heart of the English Lakeland for 150 years.' None of these cards at all would have been available in this country but for the fact that the Second World War started in August 1939, and owing to shipping difficulties a few tins intended for export were diverted to the home market. I have only two of the cards in my collection, No 1, which is titled, 'Near Ferry Nab, Windermere,' and No 18, 'Keswick and Derwentwater.' A re-run of these cards was done in 2001 and these were being put in 50 gm tins going to America. The original ones are, of course, collectors items and are valuable.

Managers standing outside the Sandes Avenue factory (now part of Baby World). Left: John Rigg (snuff manager 46 years service); Thomas Derome (head packer 44 years service) and Albert Philipson (manager of tobacco factory 40 years service)

Derek Dakeyne-Cannon

Samuel Gawith Workers

Names	Job Title	No of Years Worked	Dates	War Service
Mr F Garnett	?	40	?	
Mr J Reid	Twist foreman?	50	1863–1913	
Mr J Rigg	Snuff	60	1878–1939	
Mr C Pennington	Representative?	52	1879–1931	
Mrs Mitchell	Twist Roller	50	1884–1934	
Mr T DeRome	Spinner & Despatch	54	1884–1938	
Mr A Philipson	Factory Manager	50	1886–1936	
Mr T Smith	Tobacco Liquorer	58	1889–1947	
Miss P Benson	Cigar & Cig. Maker/Packing	52	1895–1946	
Mr W Sarginson	Spinning Foreman	52	1898–1950	1914–18
Mr W Reid	Snuff Mill Foreman	50	1904–1954	1915–20
Miss A J Harby	Packer and Stripper	47	1905–1951	
Mrs Pickering	Stripper & Pointer		1905–	Intermittent work
Mrs Fisher	Stripper	45	1906–1951	Intermittent work
Miss M Tatterson	Stripper & Pointer	40	1912–1951	Intermittent work

Names	**Job Title**	**No of Years Worked**	**Dates**	**War Service**
Miss E Noble	Cigarette Packer & Despatch	44	1915–1959	
Mrs M A Clarkson	Spinner	45	1920–1965	
Mrs A Park	Spinner, Cutter, Packer	48	1925–1972	
Mr W Routledge	Snuff Maker	49	1925–1974	
Mr W L Link	Clerk, Manager, Director		1930–79/80	1940–46 Royal Artillery
Mr A Mason	Cutter		1931–1978	1941–46 Royal Marines Commando
Mr T Hayton	Cutter, Despatch, Representative		1933–1980s	1939–41 Royal Navy
Mr D Harris	Liquorer, Snuff Maker, Despatch		1935–1990s	1941–46 RAF
Mrs W Nelson	Bookkeeper	18	1936–1954	1942–46 ATS
Mrs E Fereday	Stripper, Packer		1941–1980s	
Miss M B Williams	Cashier, Co. Secretary	21	1943–1964	
Mrs B Proctor	Cig Maker, Packer, Spinner		1944–1963	Approx ½ time
Mrs I Wilson	Cleaner		1947	
Mrs P Mofat	Snuff Packer	11	1953–1964	
Mr D Postlethwaite	Snuff Maker, snuff foreman		1953–2000	
Mr P R Ireland	Twist Dept		1956–1980s	

Workforce in the 1930s. Third left is Tommy Hughs and fourth from the right is Wilf Link. *J. Bland, Kendal*

William Sarginson celebrating 40 years with the firm in 1949. Pictured in the middle are Patricia Burgess, June Wiper and Edith Farraday.

Cutting machine – preparing blended snuff material for the first grinding operation.

Three pestle mortar in foreground with old four pestle mill in background.

Douglas Harris

Douglas Harris in the mill.

The only other pre-war incident in the life of Samuel Gawith and Company that I can record is that in the year 1935, Douglas Harris, a young lad of fourteen, started work in the firm's packing department. He progressed from there to the cutting room and then into the mill. During the Second World War he flew in forty-seven bombing missions as aimer and radar operator. During these war years, when on leave he would return to the firm and help out. In 1960 he left the mill and went into the offices and in 1979 was promoted to managing director of the firm.

The miners' strike in the early 1980s forced the company to cut back production for a time and this was followed by a threatened takeover bid for the firm which helped to distribute Gawith's snuff.

The company came through this bad patch. Mr Harris was quoted as saying, 'That other European countries produced snuff but they couldn't match the Kendal product.' In an article in the Westmorland Gazette of 27 December 1985, Mr Harris, a keen advocate of snuff and still working part-time quoted, 'Smokers should also consider changing to snuff – as according to research published in the medical journal Lancet, snuff is the best way to get your daily dose of nicotine.' At this time he had celebrated 50 years service with the firm and received a watch and dinner held in his honour in the New Year.

In 1953 Mr Samuel Anderson Gawith (Samuel the Third) died, and his widow, Louie, was appointed chairman of the Board of Directors, Mr Dakeyne-Cannon, continuing as managing director. In 1959 Mr Wilfred Lloyd Link was appointed to the Board as a director. In 1961 Mr Link was appointed managing director on the death that year of Mr D. Dakeyne-Cannon. At the same time his widow, Mrs D.M. Dakeyne-Cannon was made a director. In 1977 Mr Douglas Harris had been appointed to the Board as a director. Then in 1979 Mr Harris was appointed managing director on the death that year of Mr W.L. Link.

Left: Edith Dakeyne-Cannon and David Postlethwaite – snuff foreman.
Below: Elsie Noble helping to hand sieve the snuff after scenting.

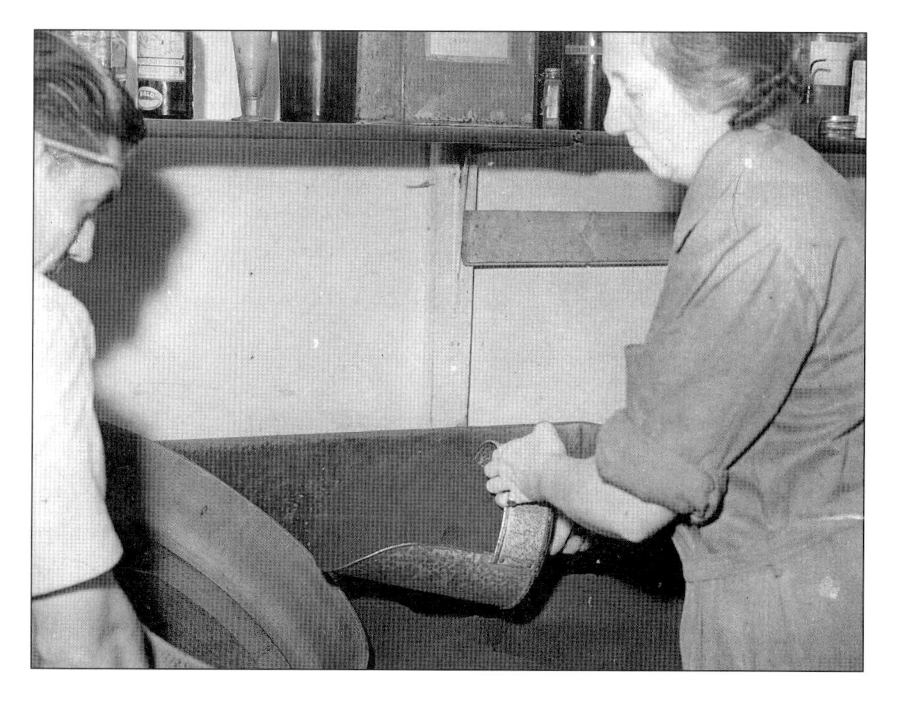

Mrs D.M. Dakeyne-Cannon

Since 1962 Mrs Edith Dakeyne-Cannon has been in charge. Her husband's mother was a Gawith. She was the only woman in charge of a tobacco company in the country and attended the prestigious 'Woman of the Year' lunches.

In 1985 Mrs Dakeyne-Cannon took on Imperial Tobacco and stopped them gaining a total monopoly of the snuff industry. The Monopolies Commission came down on her side and this was celebrated in style at the Savoy.

Here it may not be out of place to mention by name just a few of the firms products, especially, of course, the snuffs. The 1980 price list has twenty-five varieties of 'loose' tobaccos in addition to the well-known 'Finest Kendal Twist'; but the snuffs are Samuel Gawith's pride. Of these there are no less than fifty-seven varieties listed, and made by the firm. To name but a few of these we have first of all, of course, the internationally famous, 'Original Kendal Brown.' This, the oldest and still one of the company's most popular snuffs, is of the dark moist variety, and is sold plain or scented with a blend of oils peculiar to this brand. One of the drier, finely ground snuffs, is 'Golden Glow', this is 'flavoured' with menthol and a blend of scents. A popular old brand is 'Grouse Moor,' a special aromatic light snuff with a very distinctive flavour. Another noted brand is the firms, 'Dr Varey's Snuff.' This, sold in two textures, is a tobacco snuff to which is added an essence made up from an old chemical formula. It used to be recommended as a preventative against colds in the head. In addition to this last there is a range of nine varieties of peppermint snuffs, including, 'After Glow,' in two textures, and 'Mellomint,' in three textures, light, medium and dark. Five other snuffs flavoured exclusively with menthol, include 'S G Extra.' Brown Rapee, Princes Light and Princes Dark. These together with the 'Kendal Browns' are strong snuffs and should be taken with caution by a beginner. Among the more specialised and exotic brands may be mentioned, 'Scotch Black' a very coarse moist snuff, and 'Chewing Snuff' an even coarser variety, taken orally, and popular in America having firstly started in the Colonies. Other varieties include, Jockey Club, Wallflower and Lavender.

*

Left: Two women sorting and preparing the tobacco leaves before being passed on to the two other women for making into twist.

Four Mortar Snuff Grinding Mill – oldest operational in the country

The most remarkable and famous snuff mill is undoubtedly the mill brought back by Thomas Harrison from Scotland in 1792, one, it will be remembered, which he had then bought second hand as being some fifty years old. This machine is a four mortar (with a single roller pestle to each) snuff-grinding mill that has achieved national fame as a record holder. In 1965 the trade magazine 'Design and Components in Engineering' held a prize competition to find the oldest piece of machinery in the country still in regular production use. It being stressed in the conditions governing the competition, that it must be 'industrial' plant or machinery to qualify.

The competition was won, or at least the cash prize of ten pounds was awarded to a Billericay, Essex, reader who submitted and reported on this present snuff mill, which after due checks carried out by the magazine, was adjudged to be the oldest working, and still producing, piece of industrial plant in the British Isles. No one who has seen this machine could have the least doubt that it is very old, its whole construction and appearance vouch for that, and the magazine, in its article on the mill says, 'The reason we feel confident in accepting the estimate of (at least) 210 years as being the age of the machine is that the central drive bevel wheels have wedged wooden teeth. Had cast iron gear wheels been available they would most probably have been chosen as the central drive members, and since they were available about 1760 it is safe to assume that the machine dates back to about 1750.' This makes the machine at least 250 years old now (in 2003), and the remarkable thing is, that it is still working as well as it ever did, as I saw for myself just a few weeks ago. Since 1930 only two of the teeth have ever had to be renewed.

The machine's four mortars are fashioned from oaken staves in the manner of a cask but with the inward faces, around which the pestle revolves, tapering down from a top diameter of 27 inches to a mere 6 inches at the bottom. Each of the four massive iron pestles, one to each mortar, weighs an incredible 168 pounds, protruding some way out of the mortar they are about three foot in length each. Overhead, like a great umbrella, is a massive iron gear or cog wheel driving smaller gears, which, in turn, drive the shafts on which the arms are fixed which 'walk' the four pestles round the mortars. The main gear is 6 foot 6 inches in diameter, and the four individual pestle gears are about 3 foot in diameter.

'Jumbo' from Eamont Bridge Mill

The other outstanding machine is one acquired with the take-over of the Eamont Bridge Mill and brought from this last to the Kendal works. This milling or grinding machine, affectionately known to its operatives as 'Jumbo,' works on an entirely different system to the preceding machine. Jumbo carries out the grinding process by means of two very heavy rollers. Each roller, made of cast iron, is in the shape of a solid wheel some 12 inches wide and about 3 foot in diameter, and having a very smooth, highly polished tread or running surface. The rollers, mounted opposite to each other, are made to revolve round on the equally smooth floor of a flat-bottomed dish or mortar, some 6 foot in diameter. In operation the rollers walk slowly round, with their full enormous weight resting on the floor of the dish, into which the chopped up tobacco leaf (or rough ground snuff) is shovelled. Thus revolving, these massive rollers crush and grind the tobacco into finer and finer snuff the longer the process is continued.

This mill is, I understand, a unique specimen and the only one of its kind still working. I am told that it was originally designed for and used in the manufacture of gunpowder at the old Eamont Bridge Mill. As can well be imagined the process of grinding the snuff in these old machines is a very long and slow one, but at the same it is a process which adds much to the quality and the texture of the snuff, and is one which it is hard to imitate, even with the latest electronic disintegrating machines. Standing and watching these venerable, ponderous machines slowly but inexorably reducing the tobacco to snuff of the finest grade, and with my ears overwhelmed by the noise of their massive gears, rollers and rotating arms, I could well believe that Henry Wadsworth Longfellow stood thus, a hundred and seventy years ago, and then went forth from the snuff mill and wrote his immortal lines:

> "Though the mills of God grind slowly, yet they grind exceeding small;
> Though with patience He stands waiting, with exactness grinds He all."

The trade mark or emblem of 'The House of Samuel Gawith' is a patiently sitting dog, and the words 'Semper Fidelis' means – 'Always Faithful'.

The firm in 2003

The firm today is still milling snuff in the age old traditional way and the old machines are still performing their valuable job. There are now four

The old mill in 2003 with the two mixers in the foreground.

Part of the working snuff model made by Mr G. Morton from Milnthorpe in 1937 and used in various displays throughout the country.

directors – Edith Dakeyne-Cannon, chairman; her niece Helen Thornhill, Barrister; nephew-in-law, Andrew Thornhill, QC and Graham Forrest, managing director from 1990, who started with the firm in 1978, working his way up from the shop floor. The sales manager is Bob Gregory who has been with the firm for four years. They have a small, loyal workforce.

The dried tobacco leaf now comes in large cardboard cases containing about 200 kilos of tightly packed tobacco leaf. From tobacco they make a variety of mixtures, blendings, twist and flake. The two firms remaining in Kendal are the only makers of twist in the country today. Tobacco sales have been greatly reduced because of bootlegging, where tobacco is being brought in from Europe both legally and illegally. Cigars and cigarettes are no longer made by them.

When they make snuff, they put together what is called a 'mix' which is about a 100 lb of leaf and stalk and this continues through until it comes out as snuff. They produce several different kinds of base snuff. This can also be sold in bulk to other manufacturers and they can add their own mixes and label it in their own name, otherwise the firm puts their snuff into various sized tins. They do carry certain stocks of snuff but can produce as little or as much as they like at a time. They keep all the recipes in the blending room, which lists all the ingredients for all the different snuffs, together with specialised ones for individual customers.

They used to store their tobacco in the Bonded Warehouse, in Beezon Road, together with the other two companies. During the years the other companies have sold their shares and have come out of the old Bonded Warehouse and Samuel Gawiths sold the warehouse two years ago. A spur of the Kendal/Windermere railway line used to go into the middle of the warehouse for on and off loading goods.

Goods are exported all over the world, as well as being sold in this country.

Snuff Mill Today

The snuff mill is still the same. Electricity is now used for powering some of the machinery. Overhead belts and pulleys are still used. Long material tubes hang down from the ceiling and form part of the ventilation system that collects the dust and are emptied when full. The old machinery is still in place and when operational are very noisy. Bins containing partly milled snuff and waste were standing next to the old mills.

The two original 4-pestle mortars mills stood proudly with wooden protective covers over their individual pestles and mortars. On looking at the inside of the pestles the wood is partly worn away with years of usage. They are huge machines; you can just look and wonder at their size and how they were ever moved.

Jumbo is positioned on the other side of the mill and now has a covered surround for Health and Safety reasons. Large belts and wheels power it. Jumbo is used in the first stage of snuff making when the raw tobaccos are added.

There are a range of hand sieves of various sizes that the snuff is sieved through and an old wooden sided table for this purpose.

Essence Room

This is where they blend the various snuffs. The method is simple, using scales and sieves. Most flavours are produced using either one single flavour or mixing a variety together. The scent is added to the base snuff and the mixture is sieved on a wooden table. This is then put into containers. They still have many of the old bottles containing the different scents. The base snuff is kept there in barrels. White plastic containers keep the excess snuff left over from making a particular mixture.

In the old office upstairs, there are two snuff mulls and a ram's head. The ram's head date's back to 1850 and has the various appendages attached by silver chains; a small pin for freeing the grater's holes of snuff, a little rake to separate the rough snuff from the smooth, a spoon for transferring snuff from the rasp to the snuff box, and a hare's foot for brushing the snuff from the taker's upper lip.

New legislation was introduced at the beginning of 2003, stipulating that special labels should be put on all tobacco informing of the risks of smoking.

Bob Gregory and Graham Forrest.

Early picture of tobacco being transported in Zimbabwe. This picture was presented to Samuel Gawith & Co. in 1992 to celebrate their two-hundredth anniversary by Transtobac (PVT) Ltd, Zimbabwe.

Dr Rumney. *George Cole, Birmingham (late Ken Edmondson)*

FOUR

Illingworth's

John Thomas Illingworth

ALTHOUGH WE DO KNOW A LITTLE MORE about the founder of this, the second of the three Kendal snuff firms, than we do about the founder of the first, Thomas Harrison, nevertheless, John Thomas Illingworth still remains a misty figure. As in the case of Harrison, Illingworth's entry into the tobacco and snuff scene can be, date and detail wise, only a matter of conjecture. What we do know is that Illingworth was born in 1825. He would thus be some nine years younger than the man who was to be his future employer, Samuel Gawith, who entered this same scene in 1841, when, on the death then of his father-in-law, Harrison, he took the latter's place in the firm of Brocklebank and Gawith, as it became on Samuel's entry.

In this same year of 1841, John Thomas Illingworth would be sixteen, and although I repeat it is a matter of conjecture, it seems reasonable to assume that he joined the newly constituted company at about the same time as his 'boss' to be, Samuel Gawith. The mere fact that on his death, twenty-fours years later, Gawith appointed Illingworth as one of his three trustees points to a long and close acquaintance. This assumed twenty-four year long and contemporary involvement with the firm, together with its consequential parallel and shared experiences would serve to create and ripen such a relationship. This growing up together in the tobacco and snuff business, I believe, brought about the esteem and respect of the older man for the younger displayed in the trustee appointment of 1865.

An early entry into the tobacco and snuff firm is also indicated by the fact that by 1858 Illingworth was the accredited representative or commercial traveller for the firm of Samuel Gawith. A position which involved the holder in more duties and responsibilities than we associate with such a post today, as was indicated in the account, given in the preceding chapter, of Illingworth's successor in this field, Mr Pennington. I mention the date 1858 because a Post Office Directory of that date describes Illingworth as I have indicated above, and the same Directory gives us his address at that time as being, Mount Pleasant, Kendal. Mount Pleasant was a short terrace of houses at the top of Low Beast Banks, and other Directories of a slightly later date give his address simply as Beast Banks. Here, at this date, the commercial traveller, now aged thirty-three, lived with an ever-growing family of children to keep his young wife busy, especially on those occasions when the father was absent on one of his many overnight journeys.

There was a time, some ten years before this, soon after he went 'on the road' for Gawiths, that young Illingworth, as he was then, quite enjoyed these long trips with their night or two away from home. He especially enjoyed the nights that with his pony and trap, he passed at Brough, the little market town a days journey away to the north-east of Kendal. Brough-under-Stainmore was, in those horse travelling days, the recognised halting place for man and beast travelling over the lonely and desolate 'backbone of England'; the town having plenty of hotels and inns, which had for centuries thrived on this traffic.

Dr Rumney

The trans-Pennine road or A66 as we know it, runs from Brough in the west, through Stainmore Gap to Bowes in the east and the stretch between the two towns is the highest, wildest, and longest on this ancient way across into Teesside and North Yorkshire. This was all part of Illingworth's territory; but, convenient as it was for a traveller on trips to and from the east to break his journey there, Brough had other and far greater attractions for our young 'rep'. For him one bonus of Brough was that it was the domicile of one of his very best snuff customers, the town's surgeon, Dr John Rumney. The good Doctor was the third and most famous of a line of three John Rumney's of Brough, and the second of these to be the town's physician. The first John Rumney was born in 1726: the second, born in 1764, was the first Dr Rumney, and he became a noted local character, serving the little town as Doctor and mentor until his death at the age of 82.

His son, the Dr Rumney we are concerned with, was born in 1796, and after sharing the practice with his father for over twenty years, carried it on alone after the older man's death in 1846. In doing this he acquired a degree of local popularity and fame exceeding even that of his father. For this Dr Rumney had a potion or remedy all of his own, and one which earned him a lasting degree of fame which was more than local. In short he had developed and perfected a, for that time, unique variety of 'medicated snuff.' The Doctor was in the habit of buying large quantities of plain, untreated snuff (or snuff flour, as it would be called in the trade), from Gawiths of Kendal, and blending this with a mixture of medicinal oils and essences, the exact prescription of which he had worked out in secret over a long period of trial by self testing. When , finally, the Doctor had 'formulated' his medical snuff to his complete satisfaction he adopted for his motto the saying 'physician heal thyself', and dosed himself largely and often. Then, being a generous man and convivial by nature, he proffered his snuff box freely to all of his wide circle.

The result was that very quickly the taste for, and the fame of Dr Rumney's Snuff spread all over the district and further afield that the good Doctor found himself dispensing more and more of his 'panacea.'

Whether the good Doctor ever made any of his famous snuff specifically for sale, I do not know. From the widespread use and popularity of his 'invention,' we can at least be sure that many a dozen of fresh eggs and many a plump bird were exchanged against an ounce or maybe two of snuff. One way or another the practitioner had to mix more and more of his heady medicine in order to keep his growing panel of patients happy and healthy. The end result was very good business indeed, for snuff seller Illingworth, who found the Doctor's establishment ever more worth calling on, as the months went by. In fact he found that he was selling, more and more plain snuff, at the town of Stainmore Brough.

This was not all that Illingworth found so attractive about Brough and its remarkable Doctor, for to the young man the true beauty of Brough was the Doctor's daughter, the young and comely Catharine.

Marriage to Catharine Rumney

Catharine was the second daughter of the Doctor's large family and was born in 1831. This means that she could have been only seventeen or eighteen when Illingworth began calling on her father, but for all that it seems it was not long before the commercial traveller was calling on the daughter and the Doctor, selling himself to the one and his snuff to the other. As a salesman he seems to have been equally successful in selling both commodities, for soon he had established a profitable relationship with the father and an agreeable engagement with the daughter. Just when Catharine Rumney became Mrs Illingworth I have not been able to discover, but it must have been before or soon after her twentieth birthday, because the couple's first child was born in 1852, and by 1858, the date you will remember, at which we left the family settled in their home at Beast Banks, Kendal, four more had arrived.

The Children

Of these five children the first, George Rumney Illingworth, was one of the two sons that later joined the father in the family business and I will mention him again later. The second child was the one whom the mother named John Rumney after her father and her husband, sadly he died at the age of twenty-four. More happily the third child, another son, Charles Rumney Illingworth, lived to fulfil a mother's dream, and following his celebrated grandfather entered the medical profession and as Dr C.R. Illingworth practiced for some time in London, where he died in 1896. The fourth child was a daughter, named Mary Rumney, who died a spinster in 1930. The fifth child, born in 1858, was a second daughter, who was named, after her mother Catharine Rumney. Tragically she died at the age of five years and five months and it is sadly ironic to note that the two children named after the parents were the two that lived the shortest time. The Illingworth family was completed in 1860 with the birth that year of a fourth son, James Rumney, about whom much more later.

Drug Store Yard

It was at the end of 1866, or early 1867, that John Thomas Illingworth took the plunge and left the employment of Samuel Gawith & Company to start his own tobacco and snuff firm. He had secured premises at the Highgate end of one of the many yards which, in that day, ran down from the main street to the River Kent. The yard in question is, or rather was, Drug Store Yard, situated just to the south of Lowther Street. The yard was so called from the fact that from the earliest days of its existence there had been on the northern side of its entrance, and forming No 41, Highgate, a drug store. First it would probably have been a grocer/druggist shop; later it was styled a 'chymist and druggist's, and, in more modern times, a chemist's shop, which remarkably it still is today, being known as 'The Highgate Pharmacy.' In Illingworth's day the shop was occupied by a chemist named, John Taylor, and, incidentally, one of the present incumbents, R.W. & Y.J. Boyd (now retired), was kind enough to show me a prescription record book started by Mr Taylor in 1876.

There can be little doubt, that when the commercial traveller left Gawith's, he took away with him many of the latter firms customers, and some of the best. The personal rapport which the evidently efficient and popular 'rep' had built up over the years, his knowledge of his client's tastes and needs, and the friendly relationships engendered by his welcome visits to what were, in many cases, lonely households, counted for much. Many without doubt transferred their custom to Illingworth, preferring to deal with the man rather than with the firm. Prominent among these won over, or taken over customers would, of course, be Doctor Rumney and many of his relatives, friends and patients, with these latter obtaining from him all their tobacco supplies, if not all their snuff requirements.

In short he would start his business with a ready made and established body of regular customers for his own brands of tobaccos and snuffs, which in many cases he would, without doubt, 'tailor' to his clients needs. That he did this, and to his customers' satisfaction is testified to by the immediate success of the new firm. That Illingworth was on the best of terms with his wife's family (and so presumably with all the good Doctor's circle), is attested to by the naming of the snuff man's family, everyone of which, as they were born, receiving as a middle name that of Rumney, a token, surely, of great family affection.

Extended Premises in Highgate

Within a year of starting his business Illingworth found it necessary to extend his work premises, and he did this by the occupation of the shop on the south side of the entry to Drug Store Yard, across the entry from the 'pharmacy,' or No 43 Highgate, Kendal. Unfortunately Drug Store Yard, today designated 'Yard No 43,' is now but a vestige of what it originally was, being merely a narrow alley leading to the rear of the block which now covers the site of the Highgate shops numbered 43–51. No 43 now forms part of Booth's grocery store, while the rest of the block is a children's outfitters. I dwell somewhat on the restructuring of this part of Highgate because, so fast did Illingworth's business expand, that in 1869 he also acquired the shop at No 47, now swallowed up in this block. This he opened up as his main retail outlet for both his tobacco and his snuff products.

At the Drug Store Yard premises, the shop at the entry and the buildings reaching down the yard behind the shop, Illingworth had installed his tobacco roasting ovens and twist presses together with his snuff making plant, the grinding machines, sieves, and mixers. Some of these old snuff machines from these first premises were put to use at the firm's later factory, and judging by their design and construction it is safe to say that they are at least 170 years old. This means that they would be secondhand when they were set up in Drug Store Yard in 1867. It is highly probable that the ex-commercial traveller acquired them piece by piece during his last years with the older Kendal firm. Travelling around the region as he did, and with his inside knowledge of the trade he would be in an ideal position to snap up bankrupt and surplus stock items at bargain prices, and then to store them, in Drug Store Yard or elsewhere, against the time when he could see his way clear to bring them into use in his own business.

This occurred, as I have said, in 1867, and it is worth noting here that Illingworth stayed with his old firm for some two years after the death of his old principal and friend Samuel Gawith the First. As one of the latter's three trustees, no doubt played a major part during those two years in ensuring the survival and well being of Gawiths under the new management of the very young Samuel the Second and John Edward Gawith, something brought out in the preceding chapter. Only when the older firm was re-established on a firm footing and set on a steady course did he leave to set himself up in opposition.

J.T. Illingworth & Sons

During the decade and a half following 1867 John Thomas Illingworth's Tobacco and Snuff business continued to grow apace, and so too did his family. When, in 1877, the second son, John Rumney, died, the third son, Charles Rumney, was away at medical school, and the other two sons, George Rumney and James Rumney, aged twenty-five and seventeen respectively, were actively engaged in the family business. Both must have worked well and to the father's satisfaction for by the early 1880s they had entered into management and the firm had become J.T. Illingworth and Sons. Bulmer's Directory of 1885 gives 'George Rumney Illingworth, Tobacco Manufacturer. (J.T. Illingworth & Sons). Home address, 21 Strickland Place, Kendal,' from which it is obvious that George was by then regarded as a senior member of the firm, and also that he was a married man with a house of his own. The same Directory tells us, that the parents had moved from Beast Banks and that they, and presumably the children still living at home, had moved to reside at 'Fernlea,' Kendal Green, Kendal this being a then 'exclusive' residential development recently laid out on what was Low Tenter Fell, on the heights overlooking the town, just off Windermere Road.

John Thomas dies

Three years later, on the 13 June, 1888, John Thomas Illingworth died, leaving the two sons to carry on the family business, with the younger of the two, James, living together with his sister Mary and his widowed mother, at Kendal Green. Shortly after the father's death the elder brother, George, after some twenty years in the firm, sold out his interest in it to the younger brother, James, who by early 1890 was in sole control of the company. From now on for almost fifty years, the story of Illingworths is the story of this brother, James Rumney; but before continuing with this let us say farewell to George.

George Rumney Illingworth leaves

George Rumney Illingworth left the family firm and his native town to start, so I believe, his own business at Liverpool, in which city he died at the age of sixty-seven in 1920. One reason for the break in the Kendal business partnership, was a clash of brotherly temperament very much akin to that which, some dozen years earlier, brought about a similar division between the Gawith brothers, Samuel the Second and John Edward. In this connection, I believe, that James' drive and his ambitious plans for the future of the firm (including entering the cigarette, both hand, and machine made, trade) were largely responsible for the split. The older man, now with a family of two young children did not share his single brother's extravagant plans. Before leaving the subject of George Rumney it is worthy of note that one of his children lived to become Sir Gordon Illingworth, Commodore of the Cunard Line, and one time Captain of the company's flag ship, RMS *Queen Mary.*

James marriage to Mary Agnes Butterwith

Before continuing with the events of the closing decade of the nineteenth century, and the first great period of expansion under James Rumney Illingworth, let us pause to note that it was about this time, around 1890, the time when he assumed sole control, that the budding tobacco magnate married. His bride was Mary Agnes, daughter of Mr Robert Butterwith, of Denmark House, Kendal Green. The young lady would have been about twenty-six at the time, for she was born in 1864, and was thus some four years younger than her husband. The couple established their first home at No 3 Beechwood, Kendal Green, Kendal, close by the bridegroom's family residence.

Airecliffe

During the following years the union was blest by the birth of two daughters, Marjorie, who I believe, died in her early twenties, and Barbara, who, I believe left home and Kendal on marrying and becoming Mrs Tucker. She died at the age of seventy-eight in 1973, and was buried in the same grave as her parents, in Kendal. After some decade or so at the Kendal Green house, James and his family moved to take up residence in the then newly built, large house, set in its own grounds, at the north-east corner of Bowling Fell, the address of which was then simply, 'Airecliffe', Kendal. This is the house that is approached by way of Garth Heads from Beast Banks, and, being situated immediately below the Castle Howe site, looks out over the town to the east from the fell side on the west.

Messrs John T. Illingworth & Sons

Again, before detailing future events, I would like to emphasize a point that I think deserves attention. This is that although the founder of the firm, Illingworth senior, died as early as 1888, the title of the firm, beginning 'John T.' remained unchanged, in essence, until the early 1920's, that is some thirty odd years after the death of the founder, and a full thirty years after the exit of one of the sons. I say 'in essence,' however because under James Rumney's ways, and even before 1900, the old, pre 1888 title, was expanded somewhat (in line with events) to read 'Messrs John T. Illingworth and Sons, Tobacco, Cigarette, and Snuff Manufacturers, Imports of Foreign Cigars,' as a publication of around 1898 gives it.

Sandes Avenue Factory

The title, as given above, gives the clue to the direction of the growth and advancement of the firm at this period. In order to render possible and to accommodate this expansion the firm's now sole principal lost no time in putting his ambitious ideas into practice. He designed, had built, and opened in 1892, a large purpose-built factory at Sandes Avenue, Kendal.

Sandes Avenue, Kendal, on the immediate left was Samuel Gawith's, then Illingworth's. *Taken by Stengal & Co (Margaret Duff Collection)*

The then new Sandes Avenue and Victoria (iron) Bridge, built and opened in 1887, had been designed to re-route the main north/south trunk road (now the A6) through the centre of Kendal. The old, pre 1887 main road, threading the town by way of the narrow and winding Finkle Street and Stramongate and then the old, stone, Stramongate Bridge, having become quite impossible in view of the volume of late nineteenth century traffic.

Bonded Warehouse

One reason why Illingworth established his new factory on this new main thoroughfare (and also why, some years later, Samuel Gawith & Co also built here) was that immediately across the bridge (and just off to the left of the road) was also built the Bonded Tobacco Warehouse of 'The Westmorland Bonded and Free Warehouse Co Ltd', where much of the firm's raw material, tobacco (with its duty paid) was kept until withdrawn for processing. This stone building, probably finished about 1875-6 was designed by local architect, Malcolm Shaw. It is 200 feet long and 108 feet in width, two storeys in height, with its five bays, each with its projecting, roofed over, hoist, is still standing and is worth a visit from an archaeological viewpoint. The lower storey, which is composed of vaults or cellars, is fireproof throughout, and the upper storey is partially so.

Bonded warehouse in 2003.

The vaults or cellars are not sunk beneath the surface of the adjoining ground and so were safe from flooding.

The building contained sixteen commodious warerooms, four of the largest being each 100 feet in length by 33 feet in width. The building is divided into two halves by a central avenue, lighted from the roof, and containing a double line of rails, two turntables, and platforms on each side, so that goods may be received into the warehouse or despatched. The warehouses were connected with the London and North-Western Railway by means of a siding; consequently, when goods were placed upon the railway trucks in London or Liverpool, they need never be moved from the trucks until they had been drawn up alongside the warehouse.

One half of the building was to be devoted to the bonding of goods, and the other half to free goods (as many of the towns shopkeepers and traders lacked warehouse space). In accordance with Government regulations, the bonded and free departments are divided by a massive stonewall, and have no internal communications. It was expected that the bonded warehouse would be principally used at first for tobacco and spirits and also later tea and wine.

Moving back to snuff, a contemporary account in the Kendal, Windermere & Bowness Illustrated c.1900 of the man and his new premises waxes almost lyrical in its language, and is, I think worth quoting:

> 'Mr Illingworth, who is a gentleman of remarkable enterprise, and possessed of great experience in the trade, having been practically and scientifically trained to it from boyhood, resolved to build entirely new premises on the most improved modern lines, and in 1892 the present commodious mills and factory were erected, and equipped throughout with the most efficient plant and machinery known to the trade. These premises are conveniently situated in Sandes Avenue, and, with well appointed counting house and a fine suite of general and private offices, tobacco factory, snuff mills, stores, warehouses, packing and forwarding departments, etc cover a large area of ground. Every modern improvement has been introduced both in the equipments and general arrangements, to economise labour etc. and to enable the whole work to be done in a thoroughly efficient and scientific manner, the various operations being under the supervision of a specially qualified chemist and analyst. The tobacco factory is a spacious, lofty, and well ventilated building, 120 feet by 60 feet, and elaborately equipped with cutting machines, drying stoves and roasting drums, saucing tanks, steam and hand power presses, well equipped benches for spinning the roll tobaccos, and many other appliances of a highly efficient character.'

'The large snuff mills, with their spacious roasting rooms and ponderous grinding machinery also form a very notable feature. The perfection of the arrangements may be guessed from the fact that, while the works have an output not exceeded by any firm in the north, almost the whole work is done by automatic patent machinery, only some thirty or forty hands being employed. The packing department is splendidly organised, and the goods are very neatly and securely put up into cases, packets, etc. ready for immediate delivery or for transference to the capacious stock rooms. The whole of the manufacturing operations are under the constant supervision of Government officials. The Kendal Brown snuff is a leading speciality of the firm, noted for its pungency and fine delicate aroma. The firm's snuffs are carefully prepared from the dark Virginia leaf and the noted Amersfoort of Holland, and contain free nicotine and free ammonia in the most desirable proportions, while the aroma developed by their special process is of exceptional delicacy.'

Cigarette production

As will be seen from the foregoing paragraphs the main feature of this late nineteenth century expansion of the firm centred on the production of cigarettes, an entirely new line for Illingworth; but also introduced at this period was a wider range of tobaccos of the 'fancy packet' type. To take the cigarettes first, one line which was now introduced and which became very popular over the next twenty-five years or so, and this especially with the growing numbers of lady smokers, was the miniature 'Tabacettes – Cigarettes de Luxe.' These small cigarettes were not hand-rolled but were one of the first machine-made cigarettes made in Britain. They were produced in enormous quantities on a special machine, the very latest of its kind, installed by Illingworth in the new factory. Other popular, hand rolled cigarettes, prepared for sale in packets of ten, something fairly new at the time, included such brands as Wishing Gate, Sparkler, Almond Blossom and Avenue, this last name being derived from the site of the firm's new premises.

New 'Ten Packs' – Cigarette Cards – to boost sales

An innovation, which helped to boost the sales of these new 'ten packs', was the inclusion of a cigarette card in each of the packets. These, described at the time as 'miniature views of the principle places of interest in the English Lake District,' form one of the earliest 'general interest' series of cigarette cards issued in this country, and are now so 'rare' that each card is considered to be a collector's item. The cards in question are slightly larger in size than the standard small cigarette card. The picture is in black and white, with the subject title on the front or picture side, and on the back the series title, 'Views from the English Lakes,' together with 'Given with our cigarettes by J.T. Illingworth & Sons, Kendal.' The cards were issued during the period 1896-1899, and at the time of writing only three subjects are known. They are: Derwentwater and Newlands, Dungeorn Ghyll, and Wastdale Head and Great Gable. Kendal readers turn out your attics!

Fancy Packet Tobaccos

The 'fancy packet' tobaccos produced at this time by Illingworths included such varieties and brands as Gold Leaf Navy Cut; Standard Honey Dew; Wishing Gate; Peace and Comfort; Double Event; Sparkler; Navy Cut and Kendal Smoking Mixture. The Wishing Gate together with Paragon Returns and Yellow Virginia brands were tobaccos specially pre-

Wishing Gate packet of cigarettes. *late Jack Fleming*

pared for smokers wishing to roll their own cigarettes. They still also produced the older lines of the firm, the twists and the roll tobaccos (black and brown hand-spun) Irish; Cavendish and Bogie roll; the noted Kendal Shag etc.

A further feature that contributed to this period of expansion was a line of original snuffs, introduced somewhat later by James R. Illingworth. These were all based on his famous grandfather's, otherwise Dr Rumney's home-made snuff, the formula of which had come into grandson James's possession. Illingworth proceeded to commercialise this and to capitalize on it in a big way, developing a whole range of medicated snuffs, all with Dr Rumney's recipe as a base. As the manufacture and sale of these Dr Rumney snuffs continued to be one of the firm's leading lines, I will detail them, together with the more modern varieties, later.

1914–18 Surge in demand

The first two decades of the twentieth century saw an accelerating demand for all tobacco products, including Illingworth's. The war years of 1914-18 with their huge call for 'smokes' as 'comforts' for the troops. Coupled to this was the many civilian 'war workers' (many of whom for the first time were women), who could, with 'war wages', afford such luxuries, in any quantity, resulted in an upsurge of cigarette smoking. This was climaxed by the 'better life' boom of the immediate post war years, when the freedom from restraints and the abandonment of old social (and sexual) standards engendered by the years of strife and upheaval, allied to the ever increasing tensions of post war life, resulted in more and more, and younger people becoming addicted to tobacco. To meet or fulfil part of this demand, and that for his cigarette brands in particular, James R. Illingworth decided he must have far larger premises.

Larger premises – Aynam Mills

Accordingly, as soon as relaxed wartime restrictions allowed, he built and opened in 1920, a factory three times the size of the Sandes Avenue premises. In reality the new premises were two separate but adjoining buildings, hence their name of Aynam Mills. One of these buildings or mills,

Right: Aerial view of Canal Head in 1929 – showing Illingworth's in the centre of the picture, the canal head-race to the left and canal head terminus on the right.
Aerofilms Ltd Hendon / late Ken Edmondson

and by far the larger of the two, with a frontage of some two hundred feet, was the new cigarette and tobacco factory. The other building, with a frontage of some eighty feet, was the new snuff mill and office block. To this last were transferred all the old snuff producing machinery of the earlier Illingworth premises, for, in common with each of the other Kendal snuff firms, Illingworth had found that for producing certain varieties and qualities of snuff nothing can equal these original eighteenth and early nineteenth century machines.

In the case of the larger of the Aynam Mills there can be little doubt that on vacating the Sandes Avenue factory, all of the cigarette and tobacco producing plant there, was moved to and reassembled at the new premises; but this last was so large that one cannot envisage it being anything like fully-filled with plant at the time of opening, even assuming that in spite of the expense of the mammoth new premises and the cost of the move, some new machinery was purchased.

Now next door neighbours with Samuel Gawith & Company

In total the new tobacco and snuff manufacturer was so much larger than the old that, in retrospect and not being in possession of all the relevant financial facts and figures, while one admires Illingworth's confident faith in the future, one queries his business judgement. But, after thirty years in the Sandes Avenue factory during the whole time of which the demand for his products had steadily and constantly increased, there is little doubt that the tobacco 'magnate' was confident that in time he would need and use all of this vastly increased factory space. These new premises, Aynam Mills, are situated on the north side of Canal Head North, Kendal, and stretch from that road's junction with Little Aynam right the way up to Kendal Brown House, the headquarters of the older tobacco and snuff firm of Samuel Gawith & Co. This meant that the two firms, having had factories close by each other in Sandes Avenue, were now next-door neighbours at this site. In fact at this time they occupied between them the whole length of this side of Canal Head North.

Almost coincidental with the occupation of the new premises, or sometime between late 1921 and the end of 1923, the style and title of the firm was changed from John T. Illingworth & Sons to James Illingworth Ltd. Just exactly what this implied in law I am not sure, but I doubt if any particular articles were registered or the ownership base broadened, for I have not seen anywhere any reference to shareholders or directors.

Aynam Mills, Kendal 1931

Illingworth probably simply limited the firms liabilities by guarantee, but on what terms I do not know.

So we have arrived at the 1920s and the era of James Illingworth Ltd, and it seems that for some years at least, James faith and enterprise were justified. The popularity and the sales of his cigarettes and tobaccos continued unabated, while all the time the much less labour intensive snuff side of his business remained highly profitable. It was during this decade, or to be more precise, between 1924-1927, that the firm re-introduced cards, including them once more in the packets of their various brands of cigarettes. In all, four different series were issued, each consisting of twenty-five standard, small sized cigarette cards, and, unlike the pre 1900 issue, these were cards with the picture in colour. In view of the growing interest in cigarette card collecting, or cartophily, as the hobby is called, and of the fact that all of these cards are rapidly becoming scarce and hard to obtain, I will give details of each series.

Card details

The first to be issued in 1924 was a set depicting the uniforms of mounted, or cavalry regiments, each subject being portrayed on horseback. The backs of the cards give details of the history of the regiment represented on the front, together with actions, nicknames etc. It is rather a unique series, for while there are many card issues devoted to regimen-

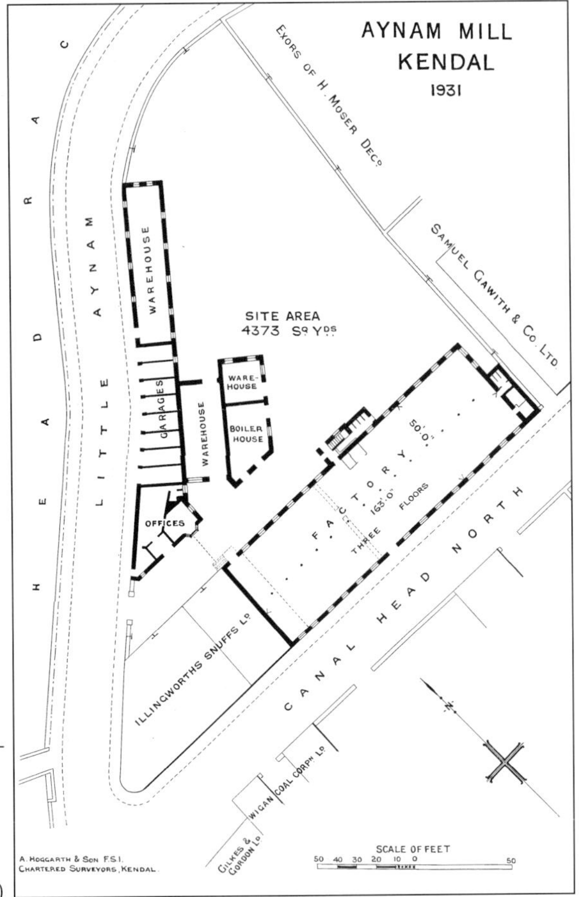

Plan of Aynam Mills 1931 – darkly outlined is the part that is being sold off. (Note A. Hoggarth & Son are the chartered surveyors)

tal uniforms, there are few concerned solely with mounted regiments. The second series is again unusual depicting as it does the fronts, or the bonnets, only of motorcars. This is unusual because although there are plenty of car sets of a general nature, few feature bonnets. This series is called, 'Motor Car Bonnets,' and I should perhaps add that only the next, or third set has a 'set title.' Issued in 1925, some of the subjects could well raise eyebrows today, No. 4, for example, where the back reads, '12/32 HP Sports Darracq. Bore 68, Stroke 110, Speed 65 miles per hour. Price of sports 4-seater £550. This car was first at Caerphilly; Shelsley Wash, South Harting and Brooklands.'

The fourth series is entitled, 'Comicartoons of Sport,' and as the title suggests, the pictures, which are black silhouettes on a coloured background, purport to be comic scenes from a range of sporting activities.

To give one example, No. 20. is devoted to Polo and the front shows a pony throwing its rider over its head between the goal posts, with below the picture the one word, 'scored!' The backs of the cards, however, give a serious and interesting write-up on the sport featured, for instance in the case of the card devoted to cricket we are informed that, 'The three wickets when in position should be eight inches wide, or rather less than double the width of the blade of the bat, which must not be more than 4¼ inches across, and its height, including the handle 38 inches etc.' The fourth series is one portraying old and famous inns of England or 'Old Hostels', as the set is called, with an appropriate description of each on the backs. This is the least unusual of the four sets.

As hinted at above the change in James Illingworth's fortune was soon to occur, and indeed did so before the end of the decade, in 1929. It must be remembered that the tobacco 'magnate' was then aged sixty-nine. Added to which he had worked hard in the business ever since leaving school about the age of sixteen and had been for practically forty years in sole control, not a bad stint, especially bearing in mind what the firm was when he took over and what it was in 1929. That, in these circumstances, he should be 'losing his grip' somewhat is hardly surprising. One can, I think, only admire him for what he had accomplished. Having prefixed it with these remarks, I will proceed to relate the story of the Illingworth 'crash' as I have heard it.

Sale of tobacco/cigarette business to Robinson & Sons of Stockport

It seems that late in 1928, or early in 1929, the firm secured a really massive order, with a prospect of repeats, for all its products, tobacco, cigarettes and snuff, from the Belgium Congo. On the strength of this order Illingworth, it seems ordered large stocks of his raw material (costly tobacco) and invested heavily in new plant and machinery; this last being probably something which he had wanted to do ever since he moved into the extensive Aynam Mills in the early 1920s. To cut a long story short, it appears that having signed contracts for the supply of the tobacco and machinery, and having taken delivery of some items, the Belgium Congo order was cancelled without redress to Illingworths. Upon this, the firm, over stretched and under-capitalised, and thus unable to meet its obligations, was forced to sell off part of its assets. In the event, Illingworth sold off the cigarette and tobacco part of his business, including premises, plant, goodwill, trade marks, brands etc., a buyer being found in the shape of the old tobacco and cigarette firm of E. Robinson & Sons Ltd of Stockport (founded in 1860), who were expanding at that time.

Snuff Mill (Little Aynam end) – Illingworth's Snuffs Ltd – 1929

By thus selling off this then major section of his business, Illingworth was able to salvage, pretty much intact, the snuff side of the business. This was located in the smaller mill, the Little Aynam end of his former extensive premises, still, nevertheless, an impressive building. The firm was then reformed and registered on the 14 December 1929 as a private limited company under the title of Illingworth's Snuffs Ltd. The board of directors of the newly constituted company consisted of James R. Illingworth, chairman; John Harold Thomas, managing director, and Mr F. Dook, secretary. We can see from the above the ageing sole controllers reluc-

DR. RUMNEY'S
MENTHOLYPTUS SNUFF
Manufactured only by
ILLINGWORTHS SNUFFS LIMITED, KENDAL
(ENGLAND)

Illingworth Label *late Robert Cottam*

tance to let go of the reins, and at the same time his grudging acknowledgement that the time had come for him to share out the onus and the burden of control and management.

John Harold Thomas – managing director

Mr J.H. Thomas, mentioned above, had entered the firm as office boy in 1903, and under J.R. Illingworth's guidance had progressed in twenty six years through the various stages of administration and management, so as to now fill the post of second in command to principal and mentor. As will shortly be seen he is destined to play an even greater part in the history of the snuff firm. Less than eight years after this reformation of his company James Rumney Illingworth died, on 23 September 1937. He was a successful business man, single-handed, and over a period of forty years, building up and running a large and complex firm. However but what strikes me, in the context of the Kendal snuff scene, is that his life was a combination of the lives of the two earlier snuff men, Samuel Gawith the First and Samuel Gawith the Second. This, I think, will be seen from the foregoing and the brief note under.

James Rumney Illingworth – the man

James was educated at Kendal Grammar School, and in his youth led a very active life. He played rugby with the Kendal Hornets Team, and was a keen member of the Kendal Cycling Club. Like Samuel Gawith the 2nd, early in his life he joined the old territorials, the Westmorland Volunteer Rifles, and must have trained under the command of the older tobacco 'baron', this last being made a major in 1878, when Illingworth was eighteen. When Gawith died in 1886 as Lieutenant Colonel of the Volunteers the younger man attended his funeral, as one of the fourteen officers present, being then a captain. Then, in middle life, and like Samuel Gawith the First, Illingworth became deeply involved in the civic life of his native town. In 1907, at the age of forty-seven he was elected a councillor. Shortly after the death of his wife, Mary Agnes, in 1910, Illingworth left the 'big house' on Bowling Fell and moved to take up residence in the smaller but very pleasant house 'West Bank', Queens Road, Kendal, which is situated across the road from St Thomas's Vicarage and which backs on to the 'Heights.' Both these residences of James Illingworth were situated in the old 'West Ward', renamed in the Boundary Review of 1919 as 'Fell Ward', and this was the ward which Councillor Illingworth represented for some thirteen years, when, again like Samuel Gawith the First, he crowned his term of civic life by becoming Mayor of Kendal in 1912–13. Finally on the 20th of April, 1923, Illingworth was made a Justice of the Peace for the Borough of Kendal.

James Illingworth

Grinding snuff. Left: Mr Robinson?; John Hutton and Tommy Fleming.
late Jack Fleming

Sieving snuff. Left: Tommy Fleming; Mr Robinson? and John Hutton. *late Jack Fleming*

Cutting tobacco leaf. *late Jack Fleming*

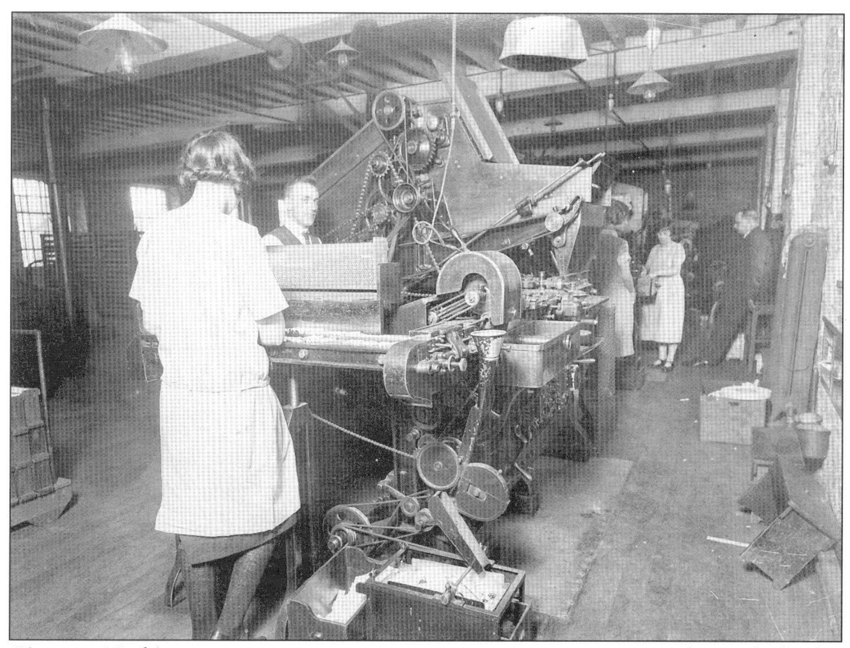

Cigarette Machinery *late Jack Fleming*

In addition the 'snuff man' was a Freemason, a past Master of the Union Lodge 129, and PPJGD of the Cumberland and Westmorland Province. As a staunch Anglican he worked hard for the Parish Church of St. Thomas and was for thirty years the Superintendent of St. Thomas Boy's Sunday School. Among the chief mourners at his funeral on 25 September 1937, in addition to his two daughters, there were two Illingworths, Miss Kitty Illingworth of Liverpool, who I believe would be the deceased's niece and his brother George Rumney Illingworth's daughter, and Mr John Illingworth of Dorking, who was, I believe, George's grandson, and the son of Sir Gordon Illingworth.

Robinson's taken over by Gallaher's – more cards

Before continuing with the history of the firm after the death of James R. Illingworth I will pause to interject a note on the next, and the final, group of cigarette card issues with an Illingworth connection. For in a way, these form a kind of 'epilogue' to the tobacco and cigarette side of the firm, and show something of the fate of the Illingworth brands in the post Kendal era. As mentioned above the firm of Messrs E. Robinson & Sons Ltd who took over the Kendal firm's tobacco and cigarette business in 1929, were at that time enjoying a period of expansion, and this growth continued with them taking over in 1934 the Manchester based firm of J. A. Pattreiouex. This last firm was founded in 1861, and amongst its brands, acquired by Robinsons were Casket, Critic, Junior Member, and Senior Service. A few years after their takeover of Illingworths, Robinson's were themselves taken over in 1937, by the powerful Northern Ireland tobacco firm Gallaher Ltd. On their acquisition of the many brand varieties and names owned by Robinson's, Gallaher's immediately proceeded to 'push' and 'up-market' certain of these brands. Among these brands selected for this treatment was the ex-Pattreiouex 'Senior Service', which, under Robinson's ownership, had gained a certain degree of popularity by the inclusion in the packets of a rather special kind of cigarette card. These Senior Service cards, as many older readers will remember, were glossy, black and white photos of medium, 77 × 52 mm size. The card series were of a high quality and very popular with smokers at the time so Gallaher's continued with them. These last extending the scope of the subjects issued (those issued under Robinson's being predominantly series of views) to include general and also unusual subjects, such as railways and, in the latter class, one entitled 'Winter Scenes'.

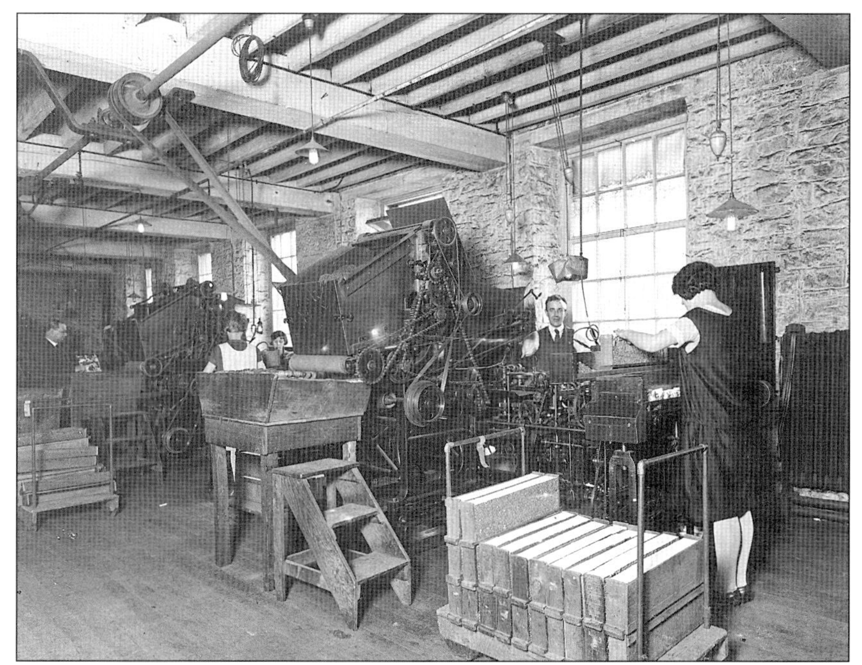

Cigarette Machines *late Jack Fleming*

Cigarette Packing. Front 2nd right – Alice Baines who married Tommy Fleming; 4th right one of the Greenbank's. *late Jack Fleming*

Cutting Department – pipe tobacco *late Jack Fleming*

Sorting the tobacco leaf. *Late Ken Edmondson*

Gallaher's issue cards for the popular Illingworth's No 10

Now another of the brands acquired by Gallaher's in 1937 and one chosen by them, on account of its popularity with the smoking public, for the new lease of life, was 'Illingworth's No 10', and a number of the 'Senior Service' type photographic sets of cards were issued in the packets of the old Kendal firm's brand with, printed on the backs of the cards, 'Illingworth's No 10 Cigarettes'. In all five sets were thus issued, and today are catalogued as 'Illingworth' issues. Specimens of these, or even complete sets, may be purchased, and although they are much scarcer than the equivalent Senior Service issues, they are still quite reasonably priced. The five 'Illingworth' sets are, with date of issue, Beautiful Scotland 1939, Coastwise 1938, Our Countryside 1938, and Shots from the Films 1937. This last was a set of 24 cards, but the other four had 48 cards to the set. All were 77 × 52 mm in size. There would probably have been more of these Illingworth cards issued but for the fact that the Second World War began in September 1939 and that era of cigarette cards came to an end.

Following the death of James R. Illingworth in September 1937, Mr John H. Thomas acquired financial control of Illingworth's and was appointed chairman on 9 March 1938. For the next fifteen years, including the Second World War years, Illingworth's Snuffs Ltd was run by Mr Thomas. However, and significantly, during this fifteen-year period three new figures entered into the life of the company, and, from comparatively small beginnings, proceeded with the passing years to play a more and more important part in the firm's affairs.

Singleton & Cole Ltd

The first two of these three men were Mr J.C. Singleton and Mr L. Waddington, who were both directors of the noted Midlands firm of Singleton & Cole Ltd. This was a public company that was tobacco, cigarette and cigar wholesalers and manufacturers and importantly snuff blenders. Here a note on the firm may not be out of place in view of the part it is later to play in the Kendal firm's affairs. The first Mr Singleton was a wholesale tobacconist at Wolverhampton who was joined by a Mr Joseph Cole. Mr Cole was experienced in the tobacco and cigarette manufacturing side, and together the two bought out the Shrewsbury tobacco business of S. & C. Harries & Son, founded in 1802, to form in 1892 a limited company based at Shrewsbury, with the intention of making their own brands of cigarettes. They went on to acquire large premises at Wolverhampton and at Birmingham as well as at Shrewsbury, and, starting as wholesalers and agents for British, American and Continental tobacco firms, they began to manufacture cigarettes on an ever increasing scale from around 1890 and up to 1914.

Illingworth's supplying raw snuff or snuff flour to Singleton's

In the meantime the company, who had always dealt in snuff, began to blend their own brand of 'Singleton Super Menthol Snuff', a line that eventually became very popular in the Midlands and enjoyed a wide sale. In time the firm found that they could not get enough of the necessary snuff flour made locally, and eventually Illingworth's came to be the major suppliers of the raw snuff or snuff flour used for the manufacture of the 'Singleton's snuff. Thus it was that the two members of the Singleton & Cole Ltd Board, and in particular Mr Waddington, who was the company's director in charge of the snuff side of the business, came to take a keen interest in their Kendal suppliers. Each acquired a small shareholding in the company and in April 1949 both were appointed to the board as directors of Illingworths Snuffs Ltd. Mr F. Dook resigned from the board at this same date. Then, his interest in the firm having grown even stronger, Mr Waddington was, in June 1952, appointed managing director of Illingworth's.

An unusual picture taken in Aba, Eastern Nigeria (note this was not posed for!) Taken by Mr. Heslop, from Kendal and working at the time for SCOA Motors.

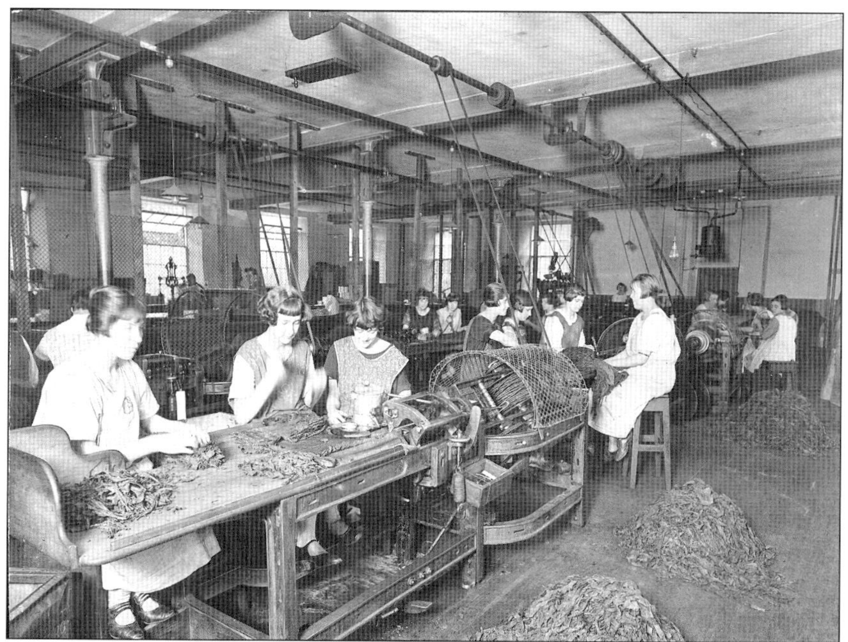

Spinning Department *late Jack Fleming*

Roll of twist in presses and boxing cut Cavendish *late Jack Fleming*

Robert Cottam

The third man who entered the firm during this period was Mr Robert Cottam, a native of Kendal, and Mr J. H. Thomas's nephew. He had been brought into the firm by his uncle, the Chairman, as soon as he had completed his wartime service in the army, the intention at the time being that Mr Cottam should train for and become the company sales manager of Illingworth's. This future, however, did not in fact materialise, as Mr Cottam himself explained. 'The head of our accounting department left to get married and somehow I moved into administration, at first in order to take over the accounting, and that was the end of my sales career, although I did spend some time in that field.'

Mr Thomas's wife, Andrina Elizabeth, died in 1940, and Mr John Harold Thomas himself died on 3 May 1953, in a hotel at Grange-over-Sands. Mr Thomas had long connections with this last place and was a life member of the Grange Golf Club. Like his predecessor James R. Illingworth, Mr Thomas was a Freemason and a member of the Union Lodge, Kendal. At the time of his death he was sixty-four years of age.

Illingworth's acquired by Leo Waddington and sold on to Singleton & Cole Ltd

On the death of Mr Thomas his major shareholding in Illingworth's Snuffs Ltd was acquired by Mr Leo Waddington, who thus became controller of the firm. However, almost immediately Mr Waddington sold all but 51 percent of the company shares to Singleton & Cole Ltd, retaining for himself a controlling interest and at the same time assuming the post of chairman of the board of directors. Following this deal the full and sole production of the snuff flour for the manufacture of 'Singleton's Super Menthol Snuff' was transferred to the Kendal firm. In this decade of the snuff firm's history following 1953 the young administrator Bob Cottam, groomed first by Mr Thomas and then by Mr Waddington, was appointed first assistant secretary to the firm in 1956, and then, two years later, in April 1958, manager. After just one years' service in the latter post Mr Cottam was made a director in 1959.

Illingworth's Snuffs Ltd, 1964 – become wholly owned subsidiary of Singleton & Cole Ltd

The next major change in the fortunes of the firm came in the February of 1964, when Mr Waddington sold his controlling shareholding to the minority shareholders and Illingworth's Snuffs Ltd thus became a wholly owned subsidiary of Singleton & Cole Ltd, Birmingham. Singleton and Cole were large cigarette importers, one of only two in the country. At the same time Mr Waddington retired from business and Illingworth's and, such was the new owners' confidence in him, Mr Cottam was at once appointed to the post of managing director of the snuff firm. Subsequent to, and consequent on this acquiring of full control, Singleton & Cole Ltd. transferred the full production, including the flavouring and the packing for sale, of their 'Singleton's' range of snuffs to Illingworth's.

This same year, 1964, Mr Bob Cottam became a founder member of the Society of Snuff Manufacturers, Blenders and Purveyors, an organisation founded to publicly represent the snuff industry. He was subsequently a member of the Society's council for a number of years and is a

T.H. Thomas; Eileen Cox; Leo Waddington, Betty Waddington. Taken by Bernard Cox (traveller for Singleton & Co) with the bonnet showing of an Austin car.

late Jack Fleming

Tommy Fleming – miller (44 yrs service) and Nellie Wilkinson – forewoman over the girls (60 yrs service) in the 1930s. Photo taken by Kenneth Sheperd.

courtesy of the late Ken Edmondson

past-president. As will be seen from the foregoing the Illingworth product plays a great part in Mr Cottam's life, in fact, as he says, while he enjoys sailing, music and gardening, snuff is his prime interest.

Cavenhams takeover – Illingworth's Tobaccos Ltd

Finally, in August 1966, Cavenhams Foods Ltd., part of the Sir James Goldsmith empire, took over Singleton & Cole Ltd. together with all their subsidiaries, and Illingworth's Snuffs Ltd, became a wholly owned subsidiary of Cavenhams, with Mr Cottam remaining as managing director. Subsequent to this involvement with Cavenhams it was decided that Illingworths should enter, or rather re-enter, the tobacco field as importers and distributors of cigarettes. Consequent on this decision and on obtaining a license the name of the company was once more changed, this time to Illingworth's Tobaccos Ltd, this occurring in April 1967. To assist and ease distribution Illingworth's acquired a depot at Chalk Farm, London. At one time every cigarette from abroad passed through their hands. A year after this, in 1968, Mr C Musson was appointed financial director, and Mr K Edmondson, who had joined the firm in 1957, was made an associate director, Mr Edmondson went on to become a full director in 1977, and was responsible for production and sales.

Ceased dealing in cigarettes in 1972

In 1972 Cavenhams rescinded the earlier decision and Illingworth's Tobaccos Ltd ceased to deal in cigarettes. Since then this Kendal subsidiary of what is now Cavenhams Ltd has concentrated wholly on meeting the ever-growing demand for their popular brands of snuff. These popular 'Illingworth's' brands include, of course, the famous 'Dr Rumney's Mentholyptus Snuff,' the first of the medicated snuffs. The brand name Dr Rumney's was also used for a range of similar snuffs, such as Dr Rumney's Export; Dr Rumney's Plus, and Dr Rumney's Peppermint, all of which featured the original Dr Rumney recipe with various additions.

Illingworth's Snuffs Ltd advertisement

The equally famous Singleton's Super Menthol Snuff, made solely by Illingworths since 1964, maintained its popularity and was in the 1970s probably the firms best seller, in the UK at least. Another proprietary brand range of snuffs taken over and made solely by Illingworth's was that of the old, Irish firm of P. J. Carroll & Co. Ltd. of Dundalk, founded in 1824. This firm is noteworthy in that in it's early mid nineteenth century days it produced along with tobacco and snuff, candles and soaps. It is also noteworthy that, although the firm is now a public company, it is still under the management of a 'Carroll,' or it was in 1970, when a new factory building was opened at Dandalk by the firm. This last range includes Carroll's Irish, Carroll's Menthol, and Carroll's Peppermint.

Trade mark – coloured rooster on a reclining crescent moon

In addition to the above special lines Illingworth's make and sell over twenty other brands of tobacco snuffs. Among these is the once very popular 'Cock of the North', the emblem of which is a highly coloured rooster poised on a reclining crescent moon. This emblem is, I believe, the nearest thing to a pictorial trademark ever used by Illingworth's. Some brands with a local flavour are 'Illingworth's Kendal Brown,' which is the firms version of the older 'Original Kendal Brown' of Samuel Gawith & Co, and 'Kenglow,' this last being a comparatively new variety developed jointly by Mr Cottam and Mr Edmondson in the 1960s, and taking its name from the firms' home town and the stimulating 'after-glow' experienced from the taking of a good sniff of this warmly flavoured snuff. Among the most recently developed is a line of 'fruit flavoured' snuffs, particularly popular in the USA, the range including, Cherry, Raspberry and Strawberry flavoured snuffs. The older scented favourites, for which there is a smaller but steady demand, include the Illingworth varieties: Bergamot; Wallflower; Rose and Lavender.

Ken Edmondson

They used aluminium containers for packaging their snuff which was safe to use for coal miners down the mines as it could not spark. Miners were one of the main purchasers of snuff, as a nicotine substitute and for clearing their airways. It was sold in National Coal Board (NCB) canteens across the country.

Workers left to right: Jack Fleming, Chris Dent, Arthur Metcalfe, Fred Mayer, Brian Murdock and Harry Booth *Late Ken Edmondson*

Kendal Snuff on the Mayflower II (1947). Showing a large wooden chest with pewter snuff boxes that were presented to Mr Wagner, Governor of New York State, when Mayflower II reaches America in emulation of the Pilgrim Fathers. One snuff box to be given to the Governor of each state in America. By Kenneth Shepherd

Late Ken Edmondson

Mill

Much of Illingworth's older snuff grinding and finishing machinery is very similar in style and construction to the old plant of Samuel Gawith & Co Ltd described in the previous chapter. This old plant, much of it acquired by the firms' founder in 1867 or earlier, was mainly used for producing the older of the firms' brands of snuff, such as the Dr Rumney range. A far more modern 'mill' with a much greater production capacity is a high-speed machine that has twenty-four beaters. These last, revolving at a fast speed, force the shredded tobacco through a series of sieves that have progressively finer and finer meshes. After milling (or grinding) in this machine the 'drier' and more modern type snuffs have their inorganic additives (it could be soda ash, potash, common salt, etc) mixed in by a modern, electrically driven, cylinder mixer. The resultant snuff 'flour' is then sieved and stored in large drums or barrels and left to mature. Later medication or flavouring takes place, when the oils, and/or essences are mixed in, this process being aided by repeated sieving. Finally the finished snuff is once more stored away for a period in barrels to allow full flavour permeation to take place.

Only after this is the 'barrel fresh' snuff packed for sale in the many and various containers called for by the particular order that is being executed. In the case of the popular Illingworth hinged lid tins, this packing is performed by a modern high speed pneumatic machine which binds a strip of special tape around the edge of the lid, this being done to ensure that the 'factory freshness' is retained in the period between manufacture and sale. The company first looked at exporting in 1946 and by 1980, 86% of the entire firm's output went for export to over twenty countries (300,000 lb of snuff per year) principally to the USA, Germany, Belgium, Sweden, Australia, Malta, Gibraltar and the Irish Republic. Least expected destination was to the West Indies, Canary Islands, Jordan and Nigeria.

The Fire

Sir James Goldsmith, the multi-millionaire tycoon, had decided in 1980 to sell all his companies in the UK and France and just continue with his companies in America. Illingworth's was on the point of sale when a fire ravaged the premises on 9 February 1983.

Chris Musson was wakened at 4am and informed of the news. Jack Fleming, works manager, attended and helped to rescue a one-ton order

Fire at Aynam Mills *Courtesy of Chris Musson*

Buckled mill workings *Courtesy of Chris Musson*

for Belgium from the storeroom. Ken Edmondson and Bob Cottam were also there to see the thirty-foot high flames spiralling from the factory, which took thirty firemen some hours to control the inferno. Fortunately they managed to prevent it spreading into the adjoining cash and carry warehouse. The building was empty and nobody was hurt.

At one point when it was agreed it was safe to do so, Chris Musson was allowed to enter the premises together with the Sub-Officer, with the sole purpose of rescuing six computer discs from a cupboard in the office which contained all their sales ledgers. This they successfully did and half an hour later the roof collapsed.

The fire had destroyed everything, including the machinery dating back to 1867, tobacco, tools, furnishings and damage estimated at between £750,000 – £1 million. Mounds of bent snuff tins and charred labels littered the floors.

Time was not wasted. Chris Musson informed Peter Franklin, managing director at Cavenhams of what had happened and was told to rebuild. The factory was insured and the instruction was to find new premises and continue. Mr Crewdson from Gilbert Gilkes and Gordon immediately offered two offices for their use. They set up temporarily that morning in Mr Musson's sitting room, with a desk and the GPO diverting telephone calls.

New Factory

The newly formed Beezon Road Industrial Estate were approached and within four weeks they had built for the company four units, 1, 2, 3 and 10. Bob Cottam was due to retire and Chris Musson took over as managing director. All the staff had been kept on and were paid weekly as key personnel by the insurers. The two other snuff firms also helped even though technically they were competitors, by allowing them use of their machinery and premises when they had finished working in the evening. Gilbert, Gilkes and Gordon built them new machines – some from designs drawn on the back of cigarette packets. There were no plans for the old machines or blue prints. Measurements were taken of some of the machinery used at Samuel Gawiths. Machinery was also loaned from Wincanton Engineering Company in Essex. For the next four weeks after 5pm each night, Chris Musson and the office manager had to go down to Stockport to process their invoices on a computer there. Computers at this time were large affairs. The firm got on its feet again in just under a month – thanks to help and generosity of local firms. The firms five sales-

Chris Musson at the their new factory in Beezon Road Industrial Estate
Westmorland Gazette
Chris Musson

man around the country had enough stock to keep retailers happy. By Easter production was back to normal.

As for the cause of the fire, no-one can be one hundred percent sure. There were various rumours (ie a lorry tampered with outside) but the likelihood of the real cause was that it started in the dust collection system. Duty at this time was £6 paid for every one pound of tobacco leaf (pipe tobacco in April 2003 is £62.03 per kilo). As much dust and sweepings as possible is reclaimed by a large vacuum system which sucks the dust up into large cloth bags 12 foot high by 15 inches in diameter which hung from a large rack upstairs. They think a spark was generated during the grinding of the tobacco, caused possibly by a small stone in the tobacco leaf. A spark of some sort was carried into the dust bags and because it was sealed it could not burn. The powder would get hotter and hotter and begin to glow, the bag would then have exploded and the red-hot tobacco powder would have fallen onto the bone-dry floorboards and together with all the essential oils the place went up like an inferno. The heat generated was tremendous and the old machinery ignited and the metal buckled. Tobacco in itself is not volatile. It was one of the biggest fires in Kendal with twelve fire engines attending.

Takeover by J. & H. Wilson

J. & H. Wilson, a subsidiary of Imperial Tobacco took over the Kendal company in 1984 – Illingworth's had a large export market and a small UK market of only 11–12 percent and Wilson's on the other hand had a large home market and small export market. Imperial Tobacco were going to incorporate Illingworth's with J. & H. Wilson's at Sheffield and were going to buy the German firm of Vitmanns, that Illingworths had successfully dealt with for many years but this would mean transferring down to Sheffield. Ken Edmondson retired about this time and Chris Musson who was now in overall charge decided to take redundancy.

Closure

Illingworth's like the other snuff firms were large suppliers to the miners in Scotland, England and Wales and was hurt greatly by the Miners Strike of 1984 and the running down and the eventual closure of many mines and other heavy industry. The firm was left in the hands of Jack Fleming who had entered the firm as a lad (4 January 1940) to work sweeping up in the snuff mill where his dad was miller. Jack as manager oversaw the removal of machinery and everything to Sheffield where J. & H. Wilson had built an extension to accommodate Illingworths.

So, sadly, Illingsworth's closed on Friday 26 September 1986 after 119 years. It could not withstand all the setbacks it had, the most serious being the blaze, which destroyed Aynam Mills, coupled with the depression in the tobacco industry and it was sadly decided to call it a day. The remaining employees managed to find other employment. For six months Jack worked for J. & H. Wilson in an advisory capacity but he did not wish to move and took redundancy. Two years later they closed and everything was moved to Liverpool.

FIVE

Gawith, Hoggarth & Company

THE ORIGIN OF THIS THE THIRD of the Kendal snuff firms is, as its very name suggests, closely associated with, and concerned with, the first and older of the three, the Samuel Gawith & Co firm. We may also note that this connection with the older firm is something which Gawith, Hoggarth have in common with the second firm, Illingworths, as was seen in the preceding chapter. The great difference in the founding of the Gawith, Hoggarth firm with the founding of both of the other firms that is again as its name suggests, the story of two men instead of one. For while Samuel Gawiths was founded in 1792 by Thomas Harrison, and Illingworths in 1867 by John Thomas Illingworth, Gawith, Hoggarth was founded in 1887 by William Henry Gawith and Henry Hoggarth.

William Henry Gawith and Henry Hoggarth Jnr.

The early connection with the older Kendal firm will be brought out and become evident as the story of the younger firm unfolds, but at the start there are one or two other and less readily obvious points which I would like to emphasize with regard to the founders of Gawith, Hoggarth & Co. The first point concerns the second of the pair, who I would like to stress is, or was, Henry Hoggarth 'junior'. I emphasize this in particular because every one of the accounts concerning the origin of the firm which I have so far read confuse this Henry with his father, Henry Hoggarth

W.H. Gawith

GAWITH, HOGGARTH & Co

Manufacturers of The Celebrated

KENDAL BROWN
SNUFF

'senior.' Henry senior was the land agent, surveyor friend of Samuel Gawith the First who when this last died in 1865 was made one of the three trustees of the deceased's estate. With Gawith's children being left orphans, he acted as a father to them, and especially so to the youngest, the then nine year old William Henry of this chapter who was the same age as his guardian's own son our Henry Hoggarth. In short the Henry Hoggarth of Gawith, Hoggarth and Company is the son of the Henry Hoggarth who was dealt with at some length in chapter one of this history of the three Kendal snuff firms.

H. Hoggarth

Background

The other point which I would like to bring out with regard to the two founder members of this third firm is how much in common they had in the early part of their lives, and, no doubt in part as a result of this, how close they became in both business and in private life. To elaborate, they had in common, of course, the Christian name of Henry, but in addition they were both born in the same year; both were younger sons of comparatively large families; they were born and raised in the same street, in fact next door to each other; both were educated at the same school and both started work at the same time and for the same firm, while finally the two were linked by the one marrying the sister of the other.

Having given this brief outline in order to show the close and parallel relationship which existed between the two founders of Gawith, Hoggarth & Co. let me now fill in the picture of the two men with a little more detail. William Henry Gawith was the youngest son of Samuel Gawith the First, the head of the oldest of the three Kendal tobacco firms. He, the father, it will be remembered from chapter one, became the mayor of Kendal in 1864 and died in 1865, so that the boy was just nine years old when he came under the care of Henry Hoggarth senior, the father of his friend Henry Hoggarth junior. Hoggarth senior, as we also saw in chapter one, took very seriously his duties as a 'guardian' of the Gawith family, and, being the oldest of the non-family trustees, acted as a father to his deceased friend's young family, consecutively with caring for his many children.

For, staying with the older man for a moment, Henry Hoggarth had, in 1850, married Miss Harriet Graham and subsequently a large family was born to the couple. The Hoggarth family, born and raised at the family house, 29 Lowther Street, which fortunatately was a large one, included five boys and seven girls. Two of the boys entered the banking business, one, Charles, becoming the manager of the Kendal branch of the old 'Lancaster Banking Company,' the branch being situated at number 70 Stricklandgate. The other of these two, Frank, I believe, also joined the same bank and became a branch manager at Morecambe. Two other brothers, Arthur and Edwin, I understand, followed the father into the land agents and surveyors business, joining him in the family firm, and, after the death of the older man carrying on the business as Hoggarth Brothers at 69 Highgate, Kendal. A daughter, Harriet, born in 1855, was the one who, as I have indicated, married 'the boy next door' who later together with her brother Henry, the fifth of the Hoggarth boys, born in 1856, founded the Gawith, Hoggarth firm in 1887.

The two Henry's the founders

To return to these last two as young people, living, as pointed out above, lives in parallel, we find that both were educated at Kendal Grammar School, both were members of the Kendal Cricket and Kendal Rugby Clubs, and that, somewhere around 1870, both started work with the Gawith boy's family firm Samuel Gawith and Company, the firm at that time being run by the two Gawith brothers Samuel the Second and John Edward. There together, for the following seven or eight years, and under the tuition of the older 'tobacco brothers',William Henry and his friend Henry Hoggarth junior, served their apprenticeship, gaining a sound and a thorough knowledge of the tobacco and snuff trade in all its ramifications. If, at the same time, we remember that while the snuff production side was located some two miles away, at Mealbank, in the old water mill there, the rest of the business was conducted at 27 Lowther Street, Kendal, and that this last was also the Gawith boy's home, we can see that in his case, and hardly less in his friend's case (living next door), their whole life was lived, if not within sight and sound, certainly well within range of the all-pervading scent of tobacco and snuff, in fact they in truth lived and breathed the stuff.

Early photograph of 27 Lowther Street *Vicky Dwane*

27 *Lowther Street*

It may perhaps be interjected here that number 27 Lowther Street, Kendal, is a much larger building than the view from the street suggests. The building reaches back twice as far as the old Hoggarth house next door, extending in fact back to the passage 'Yard No 39,' which, parallel with Lowther Street, runs from Highgate down towards the River Kent, and, with regard to this building, as was mentioned in chapter one, while Samuel Gawith the First on his death bequeathed the family business to his two older children, the two brothers mentioned above, he left the property 27 Lowther Street, jointly to the rest of his children, three sons, including William Henry, and a daughter, Jane, with the proviso that it should be a home for them as long as they each required it. The arrangement with regard to the two older brothers and the business appears to have been that they each paid into a 'family upkeep account' a fixed sum, either monthly or yearly, as rent for the business part of the premises and also, while they lived at home for their personal accommodation there. Samuel the Second being twenty-three and single and the second son, John Edward, being eighteen years old at the death of the father, who dying left his family orphans.

By the time at which we arrived, 1877/78, with the two Henrys (the future Gawith, Hoggarth & Co. partners) out of their apprenticeship, the other two 'middle' brothers and the sister had left the shelter of 27 Lowther Street (Jane to marry and become Mrs John Bibby), while Samuel the Second, the oldest brother, had left in the early 1870s on his marriage to Janet Anderson. This, significantly, left just John Edward and William Henry still living at the Lowther Street premises. I stress this last because, again as will be remembered from chapter one, the two elder Gawith brothers parted company business wise, with Samuel taking the snuff side and the snuff mill at Mealbank and John Edward, the younger of the two, taking the tobacco side located at the family house, 27 Lowther Street; and importantly, this last, the John Edward business, failed in 1885 and together with this his occupation of the business part of number 27 ceased. This is something which was to have an important bearing on the future development of the Gawith, Hoggarth firm.

It will also be remembered in connection with his brother's failure in 1885 that Samuel Gawith then bought up (or in one sense bought back) John Edward's goodwill and share of, or rights in, the old Gawith trade marks, snuff recipes, etc., and it may be asked why did he not also buy up his bankrupt brother's plant and take over the rental of the business part of 27 Lowther Street. The situation was, of course, that Samuel Gawith & Co. had, as recently as 1881, built and equipped a tobacco factory, offices, etc. at Canal Head North, Kendal. So, apart from the matter of cost, Samuel did not really need more plant and accommodation at this time, although, as will be noted later, he probably did make use of both these at Lowther Street on a temporary and a rented basis.

***

Both employed or re-employed by Samuel Gawith Co

To regress a little, after the 1878 split it is hard to be quite sure which of the two then newly formed Gawith companies William Henry Gawith and Henry Hoggarth worked for, during the period up to the failure of the John Edward firm in 1885. I rather think, however, that they both stayed on with the latter, the J.E. Gawith firm. For one thing, William Henry would be living at home at 27 Lowther Street, with his batchelor brother and would therefore be in much closer contact with him than with the older married man. Much the same situation would have been the case of Henry Hoggarth, living at number 29 Lowther Street. Whatever the position then it seems that following the collapse of John Edward's firm, and after 1885 both of the young men were employed, or re-employed, by the Samuel Gawith Company; but not for long, for in 1887 the two Henrys joined forces to start their own business, and Gawith, Hoggarth and Company was incorporated in that year.

Founding of Gawith, Hoggarth in 1887

A number of factors contributed to the founding of the partnership at this date. One would be the void left in the local business scene by the failure of the Gawith firm in 1885, something augmented in 1887 by a second failure that I will enlarge on later. Another factor was, assuming that the two Henrys had stayed on with John Edward at the 1878 split, they would, presumably, not be so happy working for the elder brother when he picked up the pieces of the bankrupt firm that had failed while they were in it. Supplementary to this, the two were now in their thirties and after some fifteen years each in the trade they would have their own ideas of how things should be done, and all that we saw of Samuel the Second (in chapter one) indicates that he was much more inclined to give both orders and advice than to take them.

27 Lowther Street possibly rented for a time by Samuel Gawith & Co

So although in 1885 the pair were employed by Samuel Gawith it is hard to imagine that it was on a happy and a permanent basis. It is more likely, I believe, that when in 1885 Samuel Gawith acquired the goodwill etc. of the defunct firm, he also rented on a temporary basis the business part of 27, Lowther Street, together with the plant still installed there, and, employing William Henry and Henry Hoggarth to operate it, ran it as a kind of branch factory until such time as he could absorb the residue of the late John Edward business in his own set-up at Kendal Brown House. One reason I have for suggesting this is that 'Bulmer's History, Topography and Directory of Westmorland,' late 1885 edition, gives Samuel Gawith & Co Tobacco & Snuff Manufacturers, Great Aynam (Kendal Brown House) and Lowther Street. It may be added that although his business had failed John Edward Gawith probably still owned some tobacco and snuff producing plant left in 27 Lowther Street, and that William Henry Gawith was probably by now the main owner of the property, which had been vacated by his other brothers and his sister (or at least, being the only occupant, he would have the main say in what happened to it) and in these circumstances the short term hire arrangement suggested above would be, at the time a mutually advantageous one for all parties.

Acquired the business of Noble & Wilson

However, the most favourable factor for the founding of the Gawith, Hoggarth venture in 1887 was the condition at that time of yet another of Kendal's tobacco and snuff firms. This not so far mentioned fourth firm, Noble and Wilson were also retail tobacconists, the partnership having been founded around 1850, when the first Noble, a tobacconist with a shop at 27 Market Place, Kendal, joined forces with a tobacco and snuff manufacturer in a small way of business named Wilson. Wilson had his tobacco factory at a building in the Woolpack Yard, Kendal, and his snuff grinding plant housed in an old mill situated on the Natland Mill Beck just to the south of the town. By 1887, however, Noble and Wilson found themselves unable to continue with the manufacturing side of their business. This was probably caused by the death of one of the partners. This part of the business, including premises, plant, and goodwill was acquired by William Henry Gawith and Henry Hoggarth.

The chance to acquire such a going concern was, in all probability, just what the two Henrys had been waiting for. To start another tobacco and snuff business in a small town in which there were already three such firms, and that with any hope of success, was one thing, to take over one of the three established ones, which even if in difficulties, had premises, facilities, and at least some customers, was another. In this situation the ladder was there and they had a foot on it, and the two new owners must have been confident that with their pooled experience and expertise allied

An early 1900s picture showing a busy day in Market Place, Kendal showing Wilson and Noble Tobacconist on left with saracen above

Geoff Thompson

to their local connections in the trade they had a fair chance of building up a viable concern from what was, almost certainly when they acquired it, an ailing one. Thus like John Thomas Illingworth before them the two partners left the old 'parent' firm of Samuel Gawith & Co and the new firm of Gawith, Hoggarth and Company was born.

In passing it may be mentioned here that No 27 Market Place (now 21a), Kendal, is still, today, a tobacconist business, carried on now by G.A. Grassings. The shop had until a few years ago a glass panelled inner door on one of the panes of which in frosted letters read the word 'Noble'.

Woolpack Yard

The two Wilson premises, which the new firm took over in 1887, are such interesting parts of old Kendal as to warrant more than a passing word. First the tobacco and snuff works in the Woolpack Yard. This last, with the ancient Woolpack Hotel (now gone and a fast food restaurant at its entrance), forms one of the largest and most renowned of the 'Kendal Yards', and busy as it is today it was even busier and more important in the nineteenth century. Then, once inside the narrow entrance, it widened out and reached so far back as to form one of the main commercial streets of the town. The Yard is situated on the west side of Stricklandgate, just south of and across from Market Place, and from the main street and is entered by a notably high archway running under the hotel. I say 'notably high' because the Woolpack Hotel and the archway were rebuilt in 1781 when this last was enlarged considerably to give space to the great 'carrier's wagons' which at the height of the horse-drawn vehicle age passed through it on their way into and out of the Yard. These massive freight wagons, pulled by a team of four horses and with white smocked attendant carriers, were long but comparatively narrow. They had to be narrow in order to negotiate these archways and entrances common then not only in Kendal but in most towns and cities, and also on account of the many very narrow bridges, a legacy of the only a little earlier 'pack horse' age, but what contributed much to the restricted width of these carts was the width of their wheels. These large wheels were being each some fifteen inches wide, and shod, three parallel iron bands each five inches in width, something which added almost a yard to the wagon's overall width.

Within the precincts of the Woolpack Yard there were then, some fifty different properties lining the two sides, some of these being quite large buildings. For example, near to the head of the yard and on the south side there was what had been until 1823 the Kendal Theatre Royal. This building, an extremely versatile structure, served after 1823 as the United Presbyterian Church, an Industrial School for Boys, where 300 boys were trained to make such local trade requisites as the wired wool combs for the wool industry, a dancing academy, and the meeting place of the Church of Christ Scientists. Across the top of the yard was a large blacksmiths forge, a busy place in those days, and, on the north side of the yard and almost up to the forge, was the tobacco manufactory. Here it was that Messrs Gawith, Hoggarth & Co began to make their tobacco and blend their snuff.

Natland Beck Mill

To grind or make their snuff Noble and Wilson had rented, or had sublet to them, part of an old watermill, where they had installed their plant, this last forming the second of the assets acquired by Gawith, Hoggarth in 1887. The mill has been converted into a house and is situated on Natland Mill Beck Lane, which lies between the main A65 and Natland Road. The mill was driven by Natland Mill Beck, the same stream that used to feed the 1740 snuff mill, higher up the beck, and is mentioned in the introduction. The mill, known as the Natland Beck Mill, is the last of a succession of mills on this site. 'Records of Kendale', By W. Farrer and edited by J.F. Curwen, 1923–26, quotes:

> '1190-1200 Gilbert son of Roger Fitz-Reinfred confirms to Gervase de Aincurt the land which Wm D. Lancastre, father of Helewise, the grantor's wife gave to him, namely Natalaund ...with licence to make a mill on the water course by the gallows of Kirkeby between Kirkeby and Natalaund,' and 1292 Natland. Robert the Miller.'

With reference to the Kirkeby (in Kendale) gallows, the town gallows were usually sited on the boundary, and the hill immediately to the north of the mill is still called Gallowbarrow and houses are built on it.

As far as is known this Natland Beck Mill was always a corn mill, and during the tenancy of Noble and Wilson, the owners were first David Galbraith and then, from 1879 to 1885, John Elleray. The mill at this time had four pairs of grinding stones or mills, and it appears that Noble and Wilson rented from 1852–1887 two of the corn mill complexes in which they had substituted their snuff grinding plant for the mill stones. This watermill is a very interesting one in that it is sited on the other side of the

Natland Beck Mill – left at back and the canal in the foreground.
Local Studies Section, Kendal Library (CCC)

lane from the stream which supplied its motive power, and apparently the feed for the mill wheel was 'picked up' at a point higher up the beck, in both distance and height and conveyed to the wheel by means of a large, twelve or fifteen inch bore, pipe made of cast iron. This pipe passed under the lane and then rose some six feet above ground level at the end of the mill and arched over to overshoot the mill wheel. The wheel frame, or housing, with the exposed part of the great pipe surmounting it, is still in place between the low wall of the lane and the mill building. The wheel housing is made of iron and indicates a wheel of some twenty feet in diameter; with a width only slightly more than that of the pipe, say eighteen inches. I imagine that the wheel would also have been an iron one, but of this there is now no trace. All but about three feet of the wheel housing is below the level of the lane, and as the wall of the mill is so near to the lane one has to peer over the wall to view the site of the water wheel and the sluice running away to the beck, which has passed under the lane a little way down towards the River Kent from the mill. According to Somervell's 'Water Power Mills of South Westmorland' (1930), the old grinding machinery left in the mill was taken out about 1910, when the waterwheel was put to work turning a dynamo used to generate electric lighting for Helme Lodge, the neighbouring big house.

With the mill situated just above the canal bridge, the mill must have received an added importance when the canal was opened in 1819 and provided a wharf within a stone's throw of the mill.

In 1887, as far as I can ascertain, Noble and Wilson and following them Gawith, Hoggarth were the only ones using the Natland Beck Mill. This meant that the two new snuff makers would, unaided, have the task of keeping the wheel running, which can be quite a heavy and time consuming task in the case of a mill fed by a leat or a diverted water supply, and one in the actual present case complicated by the piped nature of the feed. Again in this particular case the water supply itself was not from a full flowing river but from a beck, a mere stream, and that one which from my own observations could vary considerably in flow, an added problem in dry spells. It is true that there was a mill dam, but it was small, and what was worse it was a long way away (up the stream, across the Burton Road and almost up to the Oxenholme Road), and altogether, I imagine, the new firm were not very happy with the Natland Beck set up. It is hardly surprising then that within a year Gawith and Hoggarth had moved out and had reinstalled their plant in another water mill.

Helsington Laithes Mills

The move, to the Helsington Laithes Mills (there were two mills at this time) was, distance wise, a short one of some half of a mile to the south-west. The Helsington Laithes Mills are situated on the west bank of the River Kent, and are approached via Scroggs Lane, a narrow lane that leaves the main Kendal to Lancaster road (A6) some one mile south of Kendal. The site itself is just south of the great loop in the Kent that is known as Watercrook, and it is within sight of the remains of the Roman Fort of Alavna which lies within the 'crook'. The first Helsington Mill was probably built soon after the first Natland Beck Mill, for a deed dated 1297 confirms a charter of Margaret de Ros.

> '...granting in fee simple to Marmduke de Twenge, her nephew, the manor of Helsington with demesne there, the Meadow park, mill, and tenants of Helsington.'

There are later references to mills at Helsington, but by the time of the eighteenth century the site appears to have become nothing but a ruin. Then towards the end of that century a Kendal architect, Francis Webster, built, or rebuilt, on the site not one but two water driven mills, together with, just up river, a weir to feed an improved water supply through an enlarged mill race. The story is that Webster, who was a partner in the architects and builders firm of Webster & Holmes of Kendal, had the two mills built to accommodate a separate venture, one which he had developed or evolved from his use in his building plans of ornamental dressed stone, and in particular marble. The use being for property facades and, interiorly, for fireplaces etc. The 'History, Directory and Gazetteer of Cumberland and Westmorland' of 1829 says;

> 'The late Mr Webster, Architect, constructed machinery on the River Kent for sawing and polishing marble. The surrounding mountainous district supplies the finest black and other marbles, and the advantage possessed by Kendal of sea and inland navigation facilitates the importation of Italian marble to be here manufactured and reshipped to most of the principal towns in the kingdom. The limestone of Kendal Fell, of which the town is mostly built, was first polished in 1788, and it is very hard and beautiful, being variegated with petrified shells etc.'

The fact was that Webster built a complete Marble Works. The two water mills, close together, and driven from the same main race, formed the main part of the cluster of buildings, and, I believe that the 'small mill' which is the most northerly of the two (to the east of the main race and with the wheel fed by a branch race) was the saw mill, and the large

Early picture of Helsington Laithes Mill *Vicky Dwane (daughter of Charles Hoggarth)*

mill', built over the main race and with a large iron waterwheel driven from this, was the polishing mill, the plant where the most water would be needed. It may be added that Webster had leased the site from the family then at Levens Hall, the descendants of Colonel Grahme, were the owners. When Francis Webster died the marble works business was carried on by his two sons, George and Francis, and after their day by 1860 by Francis (junior) alone. Following the Websters the mills were owned and occupied by various other firms up to about 1883, after this date they were disused until in 1887 Gawith, Hoggarth & Co acquired the lease of the small mill. Here they installed the snuff making plant removed from the Natland Beck Mill, later adding to this other machines acquired by them, some probably from John Edward Gawith.

To complete the picture of the old 'marble works', however, some ten years after the occupation of the small mill by the tobacco firm the large mill and the rest of the buildings and yards etc. were occupied by Messrs J. Chaplow & Sons and used as engineering workshops for the maintenance and repair of their large fleet of traction engines, steam rollers, tar sprayers, threshing machines, etc. The firm used to either operate these machines themselves or hired them out on contract. They used the large waterwheel for power and to generate electricity. This business is still carried on at Helsington Mills by members of the Chaplow family as J. Chaplow & Sons Ltd. Road Contractors, but I understand that they ceased to make use of the waterwheel in the 1940s and that it has since been broken up.

William Henry Gawith's marriage to Harriet Hoggarth

To move on a little, around 1890 William Henry Gawith married his friend and partner's sister Harriet Hoggarth after what had, in all probability, been a liaison, if not an engagement, of some length. The couple would be in their mid-thirties by 1890 and had been in close contact via the man's old 'guardian' and the lady's father, Henry Hoggarth Snr, for all their young life, in addition to their living next door to each other until they married. On their marriage though they moved to set up a home at number 12, Belmont Terrace, Kendal. This left only the failed tobacco firm brother, John Edward Gawith, living at the family house, 27 Lowther Street, with the 'remnants' of his bankrupt business still occupying the works part of the premises (the elder brother, Samuel Gawith the Second, having lost all interest in both the plant and premises after the departure from his sphere of influence of his brother William

Henry and his partner Henry Hoggarth in 1887), and, in 1892, John Edward Gawith died.

27 Lowther Street – becomes factory and office to Gawith, Hoggarth Co 1893

This left the old Gawith factory and home empty of all occupancy, and, importantly, by this time the major owner of the property was undoubtedly (by process of deaths and removal of interest in the case of the other family part-owners) William Henry Gawith. As also, by this time, the latter's firm had become established and had outgrown the Woolpack Yard accommodation, it was almost inevitable that by the start of the year 1893 the Gawith, Hoggarth partnership would take over and occupy number 27 Lowther Street. This they did, and leaving the Woolpack Yard works empty, they occupied the whole of the old Gawith house as their factory and office premises, something which the building is still today.

The house next door, number 29 Lowther Street, was meanwhile the communal home of many of the members of the Hoggarth family. According to Kelly's Directory of Cumberland and Westmorland, 1897 edition, there were still living there in that year, some seven years after the departure of the sister Harriet (on her marriage) no less than four of the Hoggarth brothers. The four were Charles, Edwin, and Frank, in addition to Henry of the Gawith, Hoggarth and Company firm at number 27. However this date, 1897, is the last I have seen which gives any other than Henry as residing there, but as it was at this date, or shortly after, that Henry married it is quite possible that some of his unmarried sisters, at least stayed on with him and his bride. This bride was Mary Elizabeth Harrison, and if she kept house for any of her brothers-in-law, in addition to so doing for her husband and any sisters-in-law, it was not for long, for all the local post 1900 Directories give 29 Lowther Street, Kendal, as the private address of Henry Hoggarth, with no mention of any other.

William Henry Gawith died 1895

Before we, move on into the twentieth century it is necessary to record the death of William Henry Gawith. This took place on 4 September 1895. Dying at the age of thirty-nine he left a widow and two young children, these last being a daughter, Constance Ada, and a son, Samuel Henry, who, born in 1891, was just four years old at his father's death.

29 Lowther Street in 1908 with Henry Hoggarth and his young son, Charles Hoggarth standing underneath the banner 'Long Live our King' (Edward VII)

J. Henry Hogg, Kendal / Vicky Dwane

Portion of old post card – John Sinclair & Sons, Tobacco Manufacturers, Newcastle-on-Tyne
Written on back: *Mr John Sinclair, the senior member of the firm died in November 1895. He had snuffed Gawith's snuff for 40 years. After a few years of patient waiting – he gave Mr Hoggarth a sample order at the beginning of 1894. Clearly last words that he uttered were 'Gawith, Hoggarth & Co Snuff is the best!' Consequently G.H. & Co have done a large business with the firm ever since.*

The boy was named Samuel after his paternal grandfather, Samuel Gawith the First, who it will be remembered died in 1865 the head of the oldest of the three Kendal tobacco and snuff firms, and Henry after his maternal grandfather, Henry Hoggarth, the land agent friend of the other grandfather. In addition he shared the name Samuel with both his deceased (in 1886) Uncle Samuel Gawith the Second and with the son of this last, Samuel Anderson Gawith, or Samuel Gawith the Third, who was, in 1895, himself only eleven years old, but who was to become, for many years, up to his death in 1953, the head of the old firm of Samuel Gawith & Co. just as the four year old Samuel Henry was to become the head of Gawith, Hoggarth & Co. Ltd. from 1928. This means that from 1928 until 1953, a period of twenty-five years, two grandsons of Samuel Gawith the 1st, both themselves called Samuel Gawith, were each the head of a separate Kendal tobacco and snuff firms. Something which would have given great pleasure to the old tobacco 'baron' could he but have foreseen it.

Samuel Henry Gawith

The young Samuel Henry in addition, of course, shared the name Henry with his maternal uncle, his future and his father's late partner in business. A further interesting sidelight on the Gawith family and its involvement with the Hoggarth line is brought into focus if we note that the late William Henry Gawith, fatherless from the age of nine, was, boy and young man, brought up under the care and guidance of his father's friend Henry Hoggarth Snr, and that, history repeating itself, William Henry's son, Samuel Henry Gawith, fatherless from the age of four, was likewise brought up in the charge of his father's friend, the second or junior Henry Hoggarth, but in this last case the bonds between the two, of blood and of business, were even stronger.

The young Samuel Henry was educated at a once noted scholastic establishment that is now being rapidly forgotten, namely the 'Kendal Quaker School' in Stramongate, Kendal, later the 'National Boys Senior School'. One of the earliest Meeting Houses of the Society of Friends was built in Kendal about 1688, and the school founded and conducted by them reached the peak of its fame at the end of the eighteenth and the beginning of the nineteenth centuries, being then run by the Dalton brothers, Jonathan and John, teachers at the school until 1785, when in that year they succeeded their cousin, George Bewley, in its management. John Dalton, who died in 1844, became one of the greatest of British sci-

Wagons in 1909 filled with Kentucky tobacco waiting to be unloaded and shipped to Liverpool. *Vicky Dwane*

entists. He left the Kendal school in 1793 to take up a professorship at the Manchester New College. Dalton is noted for his research into colour-blindness, from which both he and his brother suffered and which is sometimes called Daltonism, the properties of gasses, and the atomic theory of chemical composition, among other things. Famous pupils of the school include the two John Goughs. The first John Gough, born at Kendal in 1721, wrote the standard early 'History of the Society of Friends', and other books. The second John Gough, born in Kendal in 1757, was known as 'The Blind Philosopher', having lost his sight through smallpox at the age of three. He became famous as a mathematician, geologist, botanist and zoologist. His bust can be seen at the Kendal Museum, Station Road, together with other items connected to him.

This museum, incidentally, owes its existence to 'The Kendal Library and Scientific Society', founded in 1835, with premises in Lowther Street. This society acquired the Todhunter Museum Collection and put it on display at Lowther Street, but in 1854 the Society acquired the large Maude family house in Stricklandgate and the museum collection was housed there for the next fifty years. The geological section was much

Right: Turn of the nineteenth/twentieth century picture (possibly taken in 1908 celebrations) showing a decorated float at the bottom of Lowther Street. Note the tobacco leaf draped over the front and the sarrison taking pride of place in the middle. *Vicky Dwane*

CAWITH, HOGGARTH & Co.
Manufacturers of the Celebrated
KENDAL BROWN SNUFF,
Manufactory, Helsington Mills, KENDAL.
Guaranteed pure & genuine
IN ACCORDANCE with
Act 41 & 42 Vic Cap 15.
SCHOOLS OF SCIENCE & ART

added to by Dr Thomas Gough and Mr John Ruthven, two of the earliest curators, and became, it was said, the finest local collection in the whole of Britain. Founder members of the above Society included Professor John Dalton; Robert Southey (the then Poet Laureate); William Wordsworth (who succeeded Southey in the same office); Professor Wilson (Christopher North of Blackwood's Magazine fame), and Adam Sedgwick, Geological Professor at Cambridge University.

Gawith, Hoggarth & Co 1923 – *Limited Liability Company*

Young Gawith must have been a credit to the Quaker School for he was able to leave at the age of fourteen with his education completed to the satisfaction of his mother and his uncle Henry. He immediately joined the latter in the two family business, beginning thus, in 1905, what was to be a sixty year association with the firm. In October 1923 Gawith, Hoggarth & Co. became a limited liability company, with Henry Hoggarth and Samuel Henry Gawith being registered as directors. The latter was then thirty-two years old and with eighteen years service to the company already behind him.

Pen and ink drawing of a happy monk 'O Yes, it's Beacon Light'. On back of card it reads *'To Uncle Henry' from Graham Hoggarth*

In the meantime the younger man's partner, uncle and surrogate father, Henry Hoggarth, had become a father in his own right with three sons of his own. Of these three, Frank D. Hoggarth, born in 1904, and Charles E. Hoggarth, born in 1908, were both to enter the firm, but the third son, Harry, born in 1903, died at the early age of twenty-five in the latter half of 1928. It was Charles E. who, many years later, in an interview in 1967, told how he remembered his father, emulating Mr Pennington of the Samuel Gawith & Co. firm and John Thomas Illingworth before him, and travelling all over the north of England in a pony and trap obtaining orders and collecting accounts; and how once his father was stranded for days during a snow storm on the Yorkshire moors alone in his trap.

Henry Hoggarth – civil duties

It was also during this same early twentieth century period that the father and company chief followed the example of service to the community set by the heads of his rival tobacco firms, notably Samuel Gawith the First and John Thomas Illingworth, by entering into the civic life of his, and their, native town. Henry Hoggarth was first elected to serve as councillor for the West Ward of Kendal in 1906, where subsequently, according to the columns of the Westmorland Gazette, he topped the poll there until 1919. In this last year the councillor was made an alderman, and a year later, in November 1920, Henry Hoggarth was elected mayor of Kendal and served as such for his full year. Commenting on his election to office in 1920, the same newspaper account quoted above says 'His wife will make an excellent mayoress'. Henry Hoggarth thus became the third Kendal tobacco and snuff firm head to be honoured as the 'First Citizen' of Kendal, while with him each of the three different firms became associated with this high office.

Christmas Gifts – 1914–18 War

Gifts of tobacco, mixture, twist and pipes were sent out for Christmas 1915 to soldiers from Kendal serving in the army in India, Burma, Egypt (British Expeditionary Force) and France. Non-perishables were sent out to India but soldiers in France received parcels containing perishables eg mint cake, plum cake, chocolates, oxo, toffee, together with bootlaces, socks and candles.

The monies obtained to enable these presents to be purchased was brought about by an appeal made by Mrs Argles of Eversley, near Milnthorpe, in the Westmorland Gazette of 13 November 1915. It was estimated that there would be approximately 800 soldiers to send parcels to and they needed to raise £200 in order to do this. Door to door collections were made and sixteen other towns and villages joined in.

It was a tremendous success and the ladies of Kendal packed up and sent the parcels of to the serving men who gratefully received them. A number of letters and cards written by these recipients found there way back to the office of Gawith, Hoggarth & Co and warmly thanked them for the tobacco, twist and pipes that were sent. Some soldiers had sat down and written them on Christmas day, sending their best wishes to the people of Kendal.

Family photograph taken in the 1920s showing Mary Hoggarth, Charles Hoggarth, Harry Hoggarth, Frank Hoggarth and Henry Hoggarth.
Frank Platt, The Studio, Kendal / Vicky Dwane

Henry Hoggarth died in 1928

Less than seven years after his year of office as mayor ended Henry Hoggarth, on 21 June, 1928, died, at his home, number 29, Lowther Street, Kendal. He was, at his death, as an alderman of Kendal, third in seniority. A staunch Conservative, he was until a year before his death the chairman of the Kendal Conservative Club. A prominent Freemason, he was a Past Master of the Union Lodge, Kendal, and received 'Provincial' honours. For fifty years he was a member of the Kendal Parish Church Choir. On the lighter side it was reported of him that in his youth he was a prominent member of the Kendal 'Orinoco Minstrels' (a group of people who came together to perform minstrel shows to raise money for good causes). Such was the man, who, following the untimely death of his brother-in-law and partner, William Henry Gawith, in 1895 (only seven years after the founding of the Gawith, Hogarth firm), single-handedly kept the company going, and thriving, for the following crucial twenty-five years (including the 1914-18 war years) until his young nephew, pupil

Right: Gulf Road, Kendal in the forefront, with Gawith, Hoggarth & Co stretching through from Lowther Street. *Vicky Dwane*

GAWITH, HOGGARTH & Co
MOTORS

and partner, could, under him, take up his share of the burden. It is, I think, greatly to his credit that he had so schooled and groomed his protégé that at the Annual General Meeting of the company following Henry Hoggarth's death, held in November, 1928, Samuel Henry Gawith, at the comparatively young age of thirty-seven, was appointed both company chairman and managing director of Gawith, Hoggarth & Co Ltd to succeed, in both of these offices, his deceased tutor and mentor.

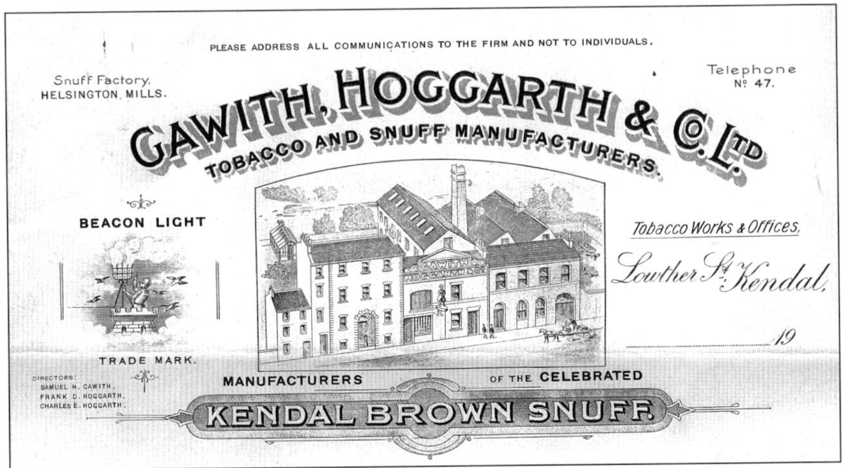

Headed notepaper

Samuel Henry Gawith – Chairman, Frank D Hoggarth – Director, Charles E Hoggarth - Director

The previous year, 1927, Frank D. Hoggarth, much to his father's pleasure, had joined the firm, and at the same 1928 AGM of the company he was appointed a director. He was then twenty-four. It would, I am sure, also have added to the deceased father's pleasure, if he had lived a little longer, to see his youngest son Charles E. Hoggarth, joining the firm in this same year, at the age of twenty and just a few months after his father's death. As early as April of the following year, 1929, at a special board meeting, Charles E. was also made a director of Gawith, Hoggarth & Co Ltd.

Now it was the time and the turn of the Gawith 'side' of the Gawith, Hoggarth association to champion and guide the Hoggarth 'side'. The time for Samuel Henry Gawith to repay in kind the care and help given by two generations of Hoggarths to him and to his father, and, as the older and the senior member of the two family firms to initiate and foster

Left to right - Frank Hoggarth, Harrison Hine, Samuel Gawith, Charles Hoggarth and Geoffrey Gawith *Margo Gawith*

the careers in the firm of his two nephews-in-law, the representatives of the Hoggarth line. His aim was to teach and pass on to them the knowledge and the skills necessary to the healthy life of the tobacco and snuff firm. This, to his credit is what the new chairman and managing director proceeded to do, thus consolidating the company. One tangible result of this was made obvious on 27 May, 1929, when, a short year after his father's death, Frank D. Hoggarth was also appointed company secretary of the firm, a position, incidentally, which one or the other of the Hoggarths were to hold for the following forty-two years.

Samuel Henry Gawith and his family

In the meantime Samuel Henry Gawith in addition to his rapid advancement in business had also been living and expanding his private life. In 1917 he married, his bride being Miss Emily Ruth Nelson, and the two established their first home at 'Runswick', Kentrigg, Kendal, which is near to the confluence of the River Mint with the River Kent. The couple were subsequently blessed with four children, a daughter, Nancy M. Gawith, and three sons. Of the three sons, Donald H. Gawith, born in 1920, became a Doctor of Medicine, the third son, Alan R. Gawith, became a Church of England clergyman, and it was the second son,

Geoffrey F. Gawith, who followed his father into the Gawith, Hoggarth tobacco and snuff business.

Geoffrey Francis Gawith

Geoffrey Francis Gawith was born in 1922, and, like his father before him, began his education at the Kendal Quaker School. On the closure of this as a 'Friends' school in 1932, he moved to finish his school days at the equally famous school of the Society of Friends at Ackworth in Yorkshire. He left there in 1938 at the age of sixteen and immediately entered the firm as a management trainee.

During the Second World War he joined the RAF in 1941 and was mentioned in despatches and received the Dutch Flying Cross equivalent to the British DFC.

Geoffrey returned to the firm after the war and in January 1946, he was appointed a director of Gawith, Hoggarth & Co Ltd.

Doris Hoggarth (temporary secretary during husband's wartime absence)

In 1942 Mrs Doris M. Hoggarth, the wife of the director Charles E. Hoggarth, was appointed temporary secretary to the company in the absence of Mr Frank D. Hoggarth on his wartime military service, and in May 1946 Mr Charles E. Hoggarth replaced the latter as company secretary.

Shake ups and retirements

In June 1958 Mr Samuel Henry Gawith, at the age of sixty-three, retired from active participation in the running of the company, but retained his office of chairman of the board of directors. At the same time Mr Charles E. Hoggarth was appointed managing director. A year after this in 1959, Mr Geoffrey F. Gawith was appointed joint managing director with Mr C. E. Hoggarth. Moving on, in 1965 Mr F. D. Hoggarth, at the age of sixty, retired from his post on the board of directors but continued working on a part time basis until he finally retired completely in the July of 1967. It should perhaps be interjected here that, although married, Mr F. D. Hoggarth and his wife had no children.

Samuel Henry Gawith died 1966

In the meantime Mr Samuel Henry Gawith had died at the age of seventy-five on the 13th of January, 1966. Although active almost to the end, continuing as chairman of the firm up to the time of his death, Mr Gawith's last year of life was marred by serious illness, and he died at the home, in West Hartlepool, of his minister son Alan. A life long member of the Society of Friends, he took an active part in the life of their Kendal Meeting House. His residence in Kendal at the time of his death was 1a Castle Green Lane. Prior to this, however he had, from 1925, lived at Kendal Green, Kendal, where it will be remembered the Illingworth family had lived in earlier times. His widow, Mrs Emily Ruth Gawith, was, in the May following her husband's death, appointed a director of Gawith, Hoggarth & Co Ltd. but sadly it was not to be for long, as she died in the October of this same year, when she was buried with her husband in the Quaker Cemetery at the junction of Sedbergh Road and Castle Green Road, Kendal.

Geoffrey F Gawith – Chairman 1966

Less than four months after the death of the chairman, S. H. Gawith, his son Geoffrey F. Gawith was elected, on 6 April 1966, to succeed his father as the chairman of the board of directors of Gawith, Hoggarth & Co. Ltd. Here it would seem is the time and place to insert a note on the family of the above gentleman, who was at this time both chairman and managing director of the company. At the age of twenty-four Mr Gawith married Miss Margaret Theressa Hodgson of 'Batlea', Underley Road, Kendal, who was then in the GPO. This was in August, 1946, and the couple began their life together at No 2 Mint Street, Kendal. Their first son, Alan J. Gawith, was born in 1948 and he is now a charted civil engineer. Their daughter, Helen T. Gawith, born in 1954, was in the late 1970s the Kendal area representative for American Express; but, as will be recorded a little further on, it was their second son, John Ruthven, born in 1949, who was to follow his father, and his grandfather, into the family business, this after receiving his education, first at the local Heversham Grammar School and then at Newcastle University.

The observant reader may have noted that John R. also follows his father Geoffrey F. Gawith being the young son who chose the tobacco and snuff field and firm as a career. The same observant reader, struck by the somewhat unusual Christian name, or rather, combination of

Christian names, of the younger Mr Gawith, may recall that earlier in this chapter I referred to a Mr John Ruthven in connection with the founding of the Kendal Museum. It turns out that Mr G. F. Gawith's maternal grandmother was a Ruthven and it seems was related to the John Ruthven of the Kendal Museum reference, who in turn it appears was quite a local celebrity of the magpie variety.

Mrs M. T. Gawith takes over as temporary secretary

In the October of 1969 Mr C. E. Hoggarth, the company secretary, was involved in a serious motor car accident, and, as a result of this, was indisposed for a long spell. During this period, and commencing in November, 1969, Mrs Margaret T. Gawith, the chairman's wife, stepped into the breach by helping with the office and secretarial work on a part time basis. Mr C. E. Hoggarth never fully recovered from the car accident and as a result was unable to resume his full time work for the company. He resigned from his post as joint-managing director, and at the board meeting of 1 January 1970, Geoffrey F. Gawith was appointed sole managing director. After serving the company in her part time secretarial post for eighteen months, and doing this to the satisfaction of all concerned, Mrs M. T. Gawith was appointed a director on a temporary, or a yearly basis, in May 1971.

Further moves and promotions

The Annual General Meeting of Gawith, Hoggarth & Co. Ltd. that took place on 4 October 1971, was an important one in the life of the company. At this meeting Mr C. E. Hoggarth, for health reasons, now resigned from his office of company secretary, and Mr G. F. Gawith was appointed in his stead, and, in addition to this, the last named was confirmed in his office of the company chairman. Mrs Margaret T. Gawith was unanimously re-elected as a 'provisional' director and at this meeting the chairman and Mrs Gawith's son, Mr John R. Gawith, was enrolled as a management trainee. It was also moved at this same meeting that the retiring company secretary's son, Mr David C. Hoggarth, be invited to join the company in a like capacity to Mr J. R. Gawith. This invitation was accepted by Mr D. C. Hoggarth and he joined the firm six days later, on 11 October 1971.

David Hoggarth in 2003

Charles E. Hoggarth retires in 1973

In April 1973, at the age of sixty-five, Mr Charles E. Hoggarth retired altogether from the company. At the AGM of this same year, 1973, Mrs M. T. Gawith was again re-elected a 'provisional' director, and this was then repeated each year until at the AGM of 1976 she was finally appointed a permanent director. At a directors' meeting held in March 1977, Mr John R. Gawith was appointed manager of the firm, and just over a year later, in June 1978, and at the age of twenty-eight, he was appointed a director of Gawith, Hoggarth & Co. Ltd. and so joined his parents on the Board.

Sole owners in 1980 – Geoffrey F. and John R. Gawith

At the end of March in the following year, 1979, Mr David C. Hoggarth resigned from active participation in the running of the company. It should perhaps be noted here that Mr Charles E. Hoggarth and his wife had besides Mr David C., only one other son, who unfortunately died in infancy. They, Mr & Mrs Hoggarth, have two daughters but they have never had any part in the Gawith, Hoggarth business. In 1980 Mr C. E. Hoggarth and Mr D. C. Hoggarth sold their shares in the company to Mr Geoffrey F. Gawith and Mr John R. Gawith. On 31 March 1989 both Margaret and Geoffrey Gawith stepped down from the Board of Directors and Geoffrey also relinquished his position as chairman. Irene Gawith, John's wife became a director on the 13 March 1981 and the company is run today by John and Irene Gawith. Geoffrey Gawith sadly died in 2001.

Firm's premises, plant and products

Mr Dunderdale concludes this chapter on Gawith, Hoggarth & Co. Ltd. with a few notes on the firm's premises, plant and products. First it may be recalled that the company's premises at 27 Lowther Street, Kendal, are remarkable in that they have been a centre of the tobacco and snuff trade for some 170 years, and, as was shown in chapter one and later in this present chapter, during the whole of that time they have been occupied by members of the Gawith family and their associates. Again it is worthy of note that during the whole of this period the raw materials used and the finished goods produced have remained the same. The end products being, of course, pipe, cigarette tobaccos and snuff.

Unlike the snuff, the flour for which is produced at the firm's Helsington Mill, the manufactured tobaccos side of the business is carried out in its entirety at Lowther Street, but, whether it be used to make snuff or these finished tobaccos, the raw material is the same, namely tobacco leaf.

Countries tobacco comes from

In 1980 the raw tobacco used by the firm came from a wide variety of sources including Malawi; Zambia; South Africa; Canada; the USA; Italy; India and Cyprus.

Tobacco Categories

From this extensive range of tobacco leaf the company produces a wide selection of finished tobaccos in four main categories. These four categories are: Flakes; Shags; Mixtures, and Tobaccos for Blending. Before going on to mention these groups individually a few general notes.

First there should have been a fifth (and a very important) category, namely the *Twists*, and in this connection there were, some fifty years or so ago (date taken from 1980), five different blends of twists forming this group produced by the company; but today only one brand of twist is made by the firm, although this does have slight variations of filler blend.

It should also be stressed, before saying anymore on this subject, that the firm does not, with the single exception of the twist, packet for sale any of its tobacco lines. The various tobaccos are sold in the main to the specialist tobacco retailers and blenders, and they are put up in one pound bags which are sold in parcels of four or more bags per parcel, with the largest parcel being of fourteen pounds.

Blending

With reference to blending (both here and with regard to the fourth of the tobacco categories), this means the blending, or mixing of different tobaccos in varying proportions by the individual customer, private person or tobacconist, to suit their own special, recipe, or taste.

Having noted the above points let us now look at the tobaccos produced by Messrs Gawith, Hoggarth, in the categories named above.

The '*Flakes*' include both the light and the dark varieties, the light including such brands as 'Bright CR'; 'Broken Scotch Cake', and this last 'Chocolate Scented', and in the dark range 'Bob's Chocolate Scented'; 'Kendal Flake', and 'No 4 Dark Scented'. There is also, allied to this range, the well-known 'Cavendish No 4' in both the black and the brown variety.

The '*Shags*' include the 'BL Kendal' (extra fine) (BL standing for 'Beacon Light', about which more later); No 4 Dark; No 5 Mixed; Dark Bird's Eye and Black. The mixtures include No 20, Latakia; No 5 (scented or unscented), and the 'cuts' – No 12, Broad; 'No 15, Medium' and 'N.O.B. Medium'.

While the 'Tobaccos for *Blending*', include such brands as 'D.V.C., Chocolate Scented; Latakia Broad Cut and No 1 Light.

The *Twist* Tobacco manufactured by Messrs Gawith, Hoggarth & Co. Ltd. is a very popular and wide selling line. It is sold in the roll (full roll or cut offs of four pounds or more in weight), sliced (by the pound), or (and) pre-packed in small packets, or pouches. In the last case (the packets) the twist is sold under the Company's well-known brand name 'Beacon Light' (in full 'Beacon Light, Kendal Twist'), and this brand name, which is also the firm's trademark, warrants a few words in view of its associations. It appears that 'Kendal Beacon Light twist tobacco was one of the proprietary brands of Messrs Noble and Wilson (and one of their best selling lines) when this firm's tobacco and snuff manufacturing business was taken over by Gawith, Hoggarth in 1887.

The older firm had apparently started making and selling the brand in 1854, soon after their foundation, and, over a period of thirty years, it had become very popular with smokers over a wide area. On the formation in 1887 of the Gawith, Hoggarth Company the new firm adopted the Beacon Light emblem as their registered trademark. The emblem it should be said, is a representation of the battlemented top of a watch-tower surmounted by a flaming brazier with its helmeted attendant. It may also be added here that in the company's main office there stands an old wooden cupboard of some four feet in width, and this cupboard is capped by a low rise pediment on which is nicely carved (in low relief) a facsimile of the Beacon Light emblem. This, in the centre, is flanked and entwined by a long twisting scroll, and on this scroll is carved the legend Est. 1854 Trade Mark Beacon Light first adopted Jubilee Year 1887.

Manufacture of twist

The manufacture of this famous twist also warrants a few words. The imported tobacco leaf is 'liquored' with water in order to soften the dry leaf, which is then left for twenty-four hours to 'case'. Next it is brought in large open boxes to the '*spinning room*', where it is particularly fascinating to watch the lady operatives 'feeding' the twist spinning machines. In front of each machine is a long table or bench upon which two ladies take the tobacco from the boxes and proceed to sort it out, setting aside the longest of the leaves for the outside, or 'wrapper' of the twist, and the shorter leaves for the 'filler' all the time smoothing and stretching out the leaves, and then passing them on, aligned up, to the third, or 'forelady'. This last, the most skilled of the team, collects and assembles the sorted leaves into an endless sausage, placing the filler material inside the wrapper leaves, while continually feeding the assemblage into the waiting mouth of the spinning machine, and doing this with a consummate skill and dexterity gained by long practice.

Originally the twist was spun on hand spinning tables, fully mechanised spinning machines only being introduced around 1928. In 1977 the present company was re-equipped with three new spinning machines of the very latest design, this in order to meet the ever increasing demand for their 'Beacon Light Twist', of which sales have again increased from that date. The twist is spun in four different thicknesses, named: Thin; Pigtail; Medium; and Bogie, and comes from the spinning machines on bobbins of about twenty-eight pounds in weight. Again the twist may be black or brown. Brown twist is ready for sale as it comes off the spinning machine, but black twist has to undergo further treatment. Vegetable oil is added to the rolls of twist, these are then bound with cloths, corded, and placed into hot plate presses, where they are 'cooked' for six hours. The following day the rolls are transferred to cold presses, where they remain under pressure for three to five days. The twist is then black and ready for sale as such.

The twist is then made into the rolls in which it is sold, or the rolls are cut-up in the packing department to be packed in small waxed paper pouches, when it is sold under the brand name 'Beacon Light Kendal Twist'. Until 1970 all the firm's twist packets were hand packed, but since then various types of fully automated packing machines have been used, and although the packets are now sold as 'priced pieces' all pieces are accurately weighed amounts. In the hand packing days it was common practice to finalise the weight of the packets accurately by including a small 'make-up' piece of twist known as a 'jockey', and many customers came to regard the jockey as a bonus, or extra over-weight piece, so that if the packet contained only the one accurately (and correctly) weighed length of twist they felt that they had been 'cheated'. This explains why, though the packing machine is quite capable of weighing and cutting off the required amount in one place, the packets still contain the small bit of twist, the 'jockey'.

Trade Signs – 'Turk'

Incidentally the pictorial design of the 'Beacon Light' twist pack incorporates a version of the traditional tobacco and snuff 'house' figure of the 'Turk', which, as mentioned in chapter one, has adorned the front of number 27 Lowther Street for the last hundred years. These tobacco and snuff blenders trade signs commonly stood at, or were affixed to the fronts of such premises in the eighteenth and early nineteenth centuries. They included effigies of Highlanders; Blackamoors; Indian Princes, etc in addition to the Turk. This Kendal example of the Turk, usually carved in wood, with a brightly painted red coat and green trousers, a long pipe in its right hand and a roll of twist in its left, was a common one, albeit with slight variations. In fact there was for many years one of these same Turk signs fixed over the door of Riley's tobacconist's shop in Market Street, Ulverston, this firm also being snuff blenders.

Turk *Barbara Ellis*

This particular design of 'The Turk' is said to have evolved from the sign displayed outside of the famous London 'Turk's Head' coffee house where Dr Johnson and other eighteenth century men of note used to take their snuff whilst drinking their coffee. Again as mentioned in chapter one, the Lowther Street tobacco and snuff figure, erected on the face of number 27 around 1870, remained there until, after a hundred years, it perished with old age. It was, however, considered so much a part of Kendal that it was replaced at the public expense. A plaque affixed to the wall under the figure says: 'The Turk trade sign, replaced by Kendal Town Council for European Heritage Year, 1975. Founded on the original that hung here for about a hundred years till it collapsed in 1973. Carved by Arthur J. J. Ayres FRBS.

Helsington Snuff Mill

The water mill and old snuff making plant was still fully operational until nearly the end of the twentieth century, and finally closed when the last

The finished article is far from sweet smelling, but the miller has a vast array of fragrances in his cupboard. The Kendal brown is a fairly heavy duty one. The favourite being menthol.

Essences are sprinkled on the ground tobacco and the whole batch is rubbed through sieves.

Blending, perfuming and packaging of snuff at Lowther Street

The blending, perfuming, and packaging of all of the firm's sixty or so brands, or blends of snuff is carried on at Lowther Street. There the many oils, essences, and spices, such as rose; carnation, wallflower, geranium; lavender; lemon; bergamot; sandalwood; cinnamon; cloves; tonquin, aniseed; vanilla; mint; menthol and camphor, are added and allowed to permeate the different brands of snuffs before they are packed (in their many and varied containers) and finally despatched to the firm's customers.

Variations in Snuff

Among the exceptionally wide range of Gawith, Hoggarth & Co. Ltd. Snuffs is the CM (Beacon Brand), which became one of the market leaders amongst mentholated snuffs. Among the older 'wet' and coarse' snuffs there are the firm's 'Kendal Brown'; Morton's' Dark Peppermint; McCombie and Western Glory. This last, a widely popular best seller of the first half of this century, is reputed to have been a particular favourite of Sir Winston Churchill. Other old favourites include the long established Prince's Mixture; Irish High Toast, and Best Barrel, while the scented snuffs include those with names corresponding to all of those mentioned in the 'flavouring' list given above, to which may be added the specialised and more exotic Sea Breezes No 27; Spartan Menthol-Eucalyptus; CM Whisky Blend; Exquisite Fleurette; Dry Orange; CM Lakeland Blend and the Peppermint Beacon Light, which did carry over into the world of snuff the company's tobacco trade mark.

The Last Miller

Alan Powley the last miller is now retired but happily recounts of his days working at 27 Lowther Street when he started straight from school at fourteen years old. He began as an errand boy in 1940 with Samuel Gawith as his boss.

Advertisement on tin displayed by shopkeepers. *Bill Moffat*

In those days there were over thirty staff at Lowther Street with four spinning machines in constant use making twist with three girls to a machine; preparing the leaf; dealing with the twists and snuff and packing everything. Monday to Friday they worked from 8 AM to 6 PM with the apprentices finishing at 5.30 PM and on a Saturday they worked from 8am to midday. The wages were not big but working conditions were good and nobody left. Alan got 12s. (60p) when he started and his wage didn't increase as fast as other firms but it was steady and similar pay to the grocery trade at that time and when they were off ill they were paid. Charles Pearson was in charge, he worked there all his life and his son took over from him but he eventually left to go to Australia.

Alan's first job was packing parcels and delivery. The choice then was post or rail. There was a morning and night horse and lorry delivery service from the railway station delivering goods in the morning and despatching parcels and crates at night. The horse knew its rounds. The packers would pack up to 500lbs worth of goods into great wooden crates that would be rolled up skids onto the lorry, and these would go off to the

Les Pearson in 1953 setting of for Australia. Taken in the packing room in Lowther Street.
Front left to right: Forrie Starkey, ? , ? Dixon, May Garnett, ? , Marjorie Dixon (Lancaster), Les Pearson, Harrison Hine (miller) and cousin of Charles Hoggarth, Libbie Noble, Iris Langhorne, ...?..... Carradice, ? , Doreen Benson and Lucy Stephenson.
Back row left to right: Alan Powley, Dennis Greenbank, Bill Shaw, Les Metcalfe, Edith Mounsey, ? ,Elsie Griffiths, Stephen Pickthal, Sarah Benson.

Westmorland Gazette / Vicky Dwane

big firms. The wooden crates were returnable. The office window at Lowther Street was bowed inwards as a result of a crate going against it whilst being hoisted up the outside, though this was not in Alan's day.

The delivery of the dried tobacco in those days was by large hogs heads, which were barrel shaped about six by eight foot. These large barrels had to be manhandled and just managed to get inside the main doors. They contained about 1000lb of tobacco. The sides were then smashed open with axes and the tobacco was put in swill baskets, to be hoisted or carried to the next floor where it was treated. The wood was later used for firewood. Bales of tobacco also arrived weighing 220lb that were of a more manageable size and were hoisted up inside and kept upstairs. Everything was manual and very hard work, the hoist being worked by pulling on chains.

Alan was thirty-six when he started paying into a pension with the firm paying the majority. When Samuel Gawith was in charge, they had factory outings every year. On a Saturday in the summer they would hire two buses that would take the workers and their families on a trip around the Lakes or to Blackpool and the theatre. Everything was paid for. The firm also paid out yearly bonuses.

During the Second World War the employees that went away were paid £1.10s.0d. (£1.50) a week and that was called a 'returner' – which meant exactly that – they would return to their old employment. There were only about three away at any one time and they would take on pensioners in their place.

Some of the women Alan remembered working with were, Mary Green; Mary Garnett; Lizzie Noble and Lucy Stephenson. Steve Pickthall was a reserve policeman during the war. Not many men worked at the factory and the young ones usually moved on. Sarah Benson worked at the factory for most of her life. Daisy Armstrong worked on until she was 80 years old - the policy being that you could stay on if you wanted to. I

Above: Works trip out on Ravenglass and Eskdale Railway in 1956. Left to right: ?, David Hoggarth, RuthWard (secretary),?, Alan Gawith and Steve Pickthall. *Vicky Dwane*

Horse Parade at the railway station with goods train in the background. Left to right – Joe Peacock, Edwin Story and George Birkett. *Margaret Duff Collection*

1953/4 – 1st Motor Parade at the Railway Station
Left to right: A Higginson (District Goods Manager), J Slater, P Gill - (winner), J Blackwood, D Turner, A Shuttleworth, N Brennand, T Conway, W Lishman, A Hill, B Bland and R S Rigg (Goods Agent) *Margaret Duff Collection*

remember she wore old-fashioned buttoned up boots and long black dresses down to her ankles.

Alan learnt how to do all the jobs; from leaf processing; learning to spin; cutting tobacco; packing; and when busy went and helped out at the mill. Everybody knew everybody else's job, especially the men.

Most of the tobacco came from Brocklebank Dock at Liverpool and brought by train to the Bonded Warehouse at Kendal. One of his jobs was to go to the Bank, the District Bank (where the National Westminster Bank stood in Stricklandgate – now the Elephant Yard) to get a certified cheque which had to be handed over to Customs and Excise at the warehouse, before they would release the tobacco. As a good deed he sometimes helped the banker carry coins out of the safe in the Bank ready for the day ahead. He remembered in Les Metcalfe's day, they wanted cash before they released the tobacco. They were very strict. There were four Customs and Excise Officers. Mr Varley from Oxenholme Road, Kendal; Alan Andrews from Barrow (one of the latter ones); Mr Pighill the surveyor (area manager) from Lancaster.

According to Alan, Mr Pighill was a bit of a character. If there was a hound trail on, he would stay overnight in Kendal, get up first thing and make his way to Ullswater by going over the tops from Kentmere, just to check the bookies!

The three tobacco firms shared the warehouse with Alexander's Brewery (wines and spirits). Customs and Excise rented offices there. The warehouse employed only one or two staff who had one set of keys and Customs had the other. The trains would shunt in backwards into the Warehouse and the wagons would be unloaded, if there were a few to be emptied, three or four staff from Lowther Street would go down and lend a hand. A Customs man would stand watching the whole time, if any tobacco managed to drop out it was all swept up.

Dry tobacco could ignite easily. When making a certain blend of snuff if you toasted it too far, it would go red and the next thing, pow and a puff of black smoke. Alan remembered in February 1962 there was a fire at Lowther Street in the drying room on the first floor. There had been steam pipes there originally but electricity was put in, there was a fault and it overheated. Luckily Mr Cragg, the baker from Riggs Bakery next door noticed the fire about 5 AM and it was quickly put out. The fire sta-

Right: Picture of Loco 45446 class 5 4-6-0 an express train leaving Kendal Station for Windermere, around 1960 showing part of Kendal Goods Yard to the right. This shows what a busy station Kendal used to be.
Taken by the late Howard Vogt, copied by Harold D Bowtell – from the Margaret Duff Collection

tion then was in Aynam Road, so they only had a few hundred yards to travel. The drying operation was then transferred to the mill.

Alan began working at the mill in 1976 and worked with Les Metcalfe for four years. Bill Shaw worked with Les after he came back from National Service in about 1953. They swapped over and Bill came and took over his job in charge of Lowther Street.

He recounts, 'I enjoyed my time down at Helsington, I worked there by myself. I used to go down and open up. You had to go under the floor and oil the shafting and light shafting, grease the main axle, open up the sluice gate, weigh everything up and maybe raise the main sluice gate. Towards the end, the dam was silting up and it was difficult to get enough power for all the machinery, sometimes one would maybe have to be disengaged, as they were not getting the weight of water down. There were four sets of equipment as mentioned. The salts were added to bring out the flavour. The drying room is where the different blends of tobacco is laid out to dry and is left there until the moisture content is down to 5% before it is put into the ball mills to produce a fine snuff. The heat comes through the performated floor and is turned manually with a fork.

The mortars used at the mill were exactly the same as the ones at the gunpowder works at Sedgwick. The machinery never failed. The three-pestle had a minor repair whereby a ring was welded down and sharp-

Presentation to mark Steve Pickthall's 50 years service.
Left to right: Charles Hoggarth, Edith Mounsey, Steve Pickthall, Dennis Greenbank and Alan Powley. *Vicky Dwane*

The special presentation of a clock (left to right): Geoffrey Gawith, Florrie Starkey, Charles Hoggarth and Samuel Gawith. *Vicky Dwane*

ON THE PAYROLL OF GAWITH, HOGGARTH & CO LTD

For week commencing 20 June 1938

Name and date of birth of employees	
Pearson, Charles A	2.4.1887
Hine, Harrison	19.1.1887
Sarginson, Nathan	26.3.1880
Pickthall, Stephen	5.7.1903
Pearson, Charles Leslie	27.3.1912
Metcalfe, John Leslie	28.9.1919
Starkey, Florence	26.12.1891
Armstrong, Eliz	18.12.1875
Rylands, Matilda	30.11.1891
Neighbour, Margaret (Mrs)	31.5.1904
Noble, Eliz	19.2.1889
Mounsey, Edith	21.1.1906
Wolstenholme, Kathleen	1.3.1913
Griffiths, Elsie	24.10.1906
Nevinson, Alice	18.3.1904
Benson, Sarah	11.1.1897
Cottam, Ethel	7.4.1923

GAWITH, HOGGARTH & CO LTD

PAY BOOK

Week commencing 20 June 1938 – 1954

Dates of Employees joining Firm or Company

		25 years	50 years
C A Pearson	June 1890	1915	1940
H Hine	June 1901	1926	1951
N Sarginson	July 1920	1945	
S Pickthall	Feb 1918	1943	
C L Pearson	April 1926	1951	
J L Metcalfe	Dec 1933	1958	
J A Powley	March 1940	1965	
D Greenbank	Feb 1941	1966	
W Gilpin	Jan 1946		
J McGrady	July 1946		
Wm Shaw	Nov 1943		
E Armstrong	June 1892	1917	1942
F Starkey	Feb 1906	1931	1956
M Rylands	Aug 1918	1943	
M Neighbour	Aug 1919	1944 (line scored through)	
E Noble	April 1920	1945	
E Mounsey	Aug 1920	1945	
K Wolstenholm	Jan 1928	1953 (line scored through)	
E Griffiths	Nov 1929	1954	
A Nevinson	Nov 1929	1954 (line scored through)	
S Benson	Nov 1929	1954	
E Cottam	Aug 1937	1962 (line scored through)	
D Wilkinson	Oct 1943		
M Dixon	April 1945		
R Beagan	July 1946		
L Stephenson	Aug 1946		
D Wilkinson	Oct 1943		
J Atkinson	Oct 1947		

*Income Tax is payable on an amount exceeding: £2.80 per week 1936-37
£3.00 per week 1949-50

Photograph by Westmorland Gazette of Gawith, Hoggarth staff in the 1960s.
Front row, left to right:- Charles Hoggarth (partner then); Lucy Stephenson; Nellie Cottam; Edith Mounsey (worked from 14 yrs old until retirement) snuff and packing; Ethel Gilpin (spinner, twist – Brown Irish); Mary Allen (maiden name) and Ruth Mason (Twist).
Charles Dobson - packing; Steve Pickthall – worked from school, climbing spare time - foreman, Denis Greenbank (behind); John Handley – worked in shed like Martin today; Edna Doughety – weighing and packing; Sheila ? ; Bill Shaw (from school was a foreman); Wendy Vickers (machine); Iris Brandle – white permed hair) - supervisor; Linda English – young lass (nee Hopper)- in office;. ? Lilly Donoghue. *Barbara Ellis*

ened. Another time a local joiner came and had to re-wood one of the mortars using hardwood. Gilkes and Gordon carried out any repairs.

Upstairs in the mill was never used, it had years ago been the home of the miller but used by them only to oil parts of the machinery via the three trap doors. He remembers many visitors, including a Russian Trade Delegation.

The snuff was then bagged and taken back to Lowther Street by Newby's for finishing off and packaging.

The firm in 2003

Things have certainly moved on, and during 1993–1994 the firm moved into three large spacious modern industrial units on the edge of town, where the old creamery used to be. They had outgrown there Lowther Street premises, but still carry on making twist, pipe tobacco and packing snuff there as they have done for over a hundred years and employ eight members of staff there, two of which are part-time. Customs and Excise had never been happy with their set up in Lowther Street. They had always wanted one room or place as a designated secure store but this proved rather difficult, if not impossible, and many little rooms had to be designated.

Another reason for the move was the purchase of a small production unit, from British American Tobacco, at Southampton, that can deal with 1,000 kg of tobacco an hour, which increased volumes considerably.

The large cardboard boxes containing 200 kilos each of dried tobacco leaf sit waiting by the side of this modern unit and the colours vary, dependent on what country they came from and how the tobacco was dried, fire or flue cured. Colours can range from lemon, orange coloured through to brown with different colours and types for different end products. The lighter colour for cigarettes – that is flue cured. The darker for twists and flake. From Cyprus, Latakia comes not in cardboard boxes but in hessian sacking weighing approximately 70 kilos. The tobacco comes from all over the world.

The dried tobacco is first put into the vacuum chamber of this unit and vacuum is drawn. Steam is pumped into the dry tightly packed tobacco and it comes out boiling hot. It is then put into a conditioning cylinder that puts moisture in to it. From there it gets layered, adding different types of leaf and when cut this gets mixed then left overnight. Then it is re-dried in the dryer and put into a cylinder for the flavours to be added. There are less staff employed with this modern equipment, which is more efficient and a fork lift truck is used to deal with the heavy boxes of tobacco leaf.

Even today the boxes of tobacco used at Lowther Street, have to be taken and unloaded by hand at the front door, a hoist powered by a small motor, lifts the boxes through a trap door and onto the upper floor, where it then has to be man-handled by two men to be stacked a few at a time. Prior to the new premises this was a continuous process, whereby the bulk of the leaf was stored at the Bonded Warehouse on Beezon Sidings and had to be moved frequently to restock Lowther Street. This was a tiresome job even at the Bonded Warehouse, as the leaf was stored on the top half, so it had to be trollied along by two or three people before being dropped down and removed. Today large container wagons deliver the boxes of tobacco, from India, Malawi, Mozambique, Tanzania and

Tobacco being processed today in this new machinery.

Uganda and it is stored, piled high in one of their industrial units ready to be moved into position, when required, by their fork lift truck, with little effort.

In October 1998 they became partners with Alois Pöschl, a German firm to form Gawith, Hoggarth Tobacco Trading to run alongside their old established firm of Gawith, Hoggarth & Co. Ltd. Alois Pöschl is the biggest snuff manufacturer in Europe, if not the world. (It was originally started by Wilhelm and Alois Pöschl of Landshut). The two firms have set up a separate sales and marketing company of which Gawith and Hoggarth are the major shareholder having a 65 percent stake. They are an international company. The German firm now sell, under licence, Gawith and Hoggarth tobacco products, as they do theirs. It has worked well and their sales reps have doubled. They also buy in their base snuff from them and blend in their own flavours. Gawith, Hoggarth also buy in other ancillary products for sale from their German partner and other UK businesses like, pipes, pipe cleaners, cigarette holders, pouches for holding tobacco and such like, which are all sold under the Trading Tobacco firm. They also buy in other well-known brands that would not be worthwhile making to sell on or distribute. There are now two designated warehouses for the purpose of Excise – one for each company.

John Gawith in his warehouse with bags of hessian Latakia behind him

They have a good range of twists, pipe tobacco, rolling tobacco and this is sold loose to specialist tobacconists or in 50 gm containers. (500 gms, 50 gms and pouches containing 50, 25; 12½ gms) Women work in modern light rooms, weighing, labelling and packaging. Some are labelled with a customers own name. There is now a much bigger range of tobaccos than in the 1980s. Snuff forms a much smaller percentage of sales but it is still important and is mostly sold in tins, though Alois Pöschl sell theirs in modern plastic dispensing containers.

Sadly the Beacon Light emblem is now no longer used anymore, the tobaccos are just known by the name 'Gawith, Hoggarth & Co. Ltd.' Small amounts of twist are sold in vacuum packed small plastic bags with the distinctive 'Turk figure.'

The Lowther Street premises remain the same. The observer is taken back in time. Nothing has changed bar the workers clothing, the sound of music from a nearby radio and some modern packaging. The old equipment is still producing the same high class goods, made over the same time span. The women work on the top floor, many having worked there for many years, four were spinning twist, two on each machine. On the middle floor the twist is wound round wheels, the thickest and smallest, waiting to be weighed and rolled into smaller sized balls. The different thicknesses now produced are pigtail (thin); Bogie (medium); Black Irish X, which is a thick twist and the extra large is called the Black Irish XXX.

Martin Davies, the deputy charge-hand of eighteen years, explained how the raw leaf had been hoisted up from downstairs, and put in the steamer and the different variations of timings required to make the tobacco moist and pliable. This reconstituted tobacco now lay-on the age-old floor boards in heaps, with pieces of canvas covering the mounds to keep the moisture in. Dave Nightingale, who has been with the company for twenty-seven years, manufactures the flakes, helps with the twists and maintenance of the machinery. He explained that the brown twist was put into cold presses but the black had been coated in vegetable oil and cooked in the old steam presses on the ground floor and was milder when cooked and coming out black. One of his jobs was rolling the twist into baseball-sized balls ready for storing. Some of the different flavourings for twist are apple, strawberry, aniseed and black cherry.

Downstairs, the goods are packed and wait to go out, when they will be taken back to the modern factory for storage and distribution. A room on the left as you go in at the front door, is the old office, with the cupboard facing with the wood carving on the uppermost part displaying the old Beacon Light emblem. The office is sadly no longer used and has been overtaken by the new computerised office with four people in at the other site. Along the passage is Barbara Ellis who has been with the firm for nearly thirty-two years, and does the weighing and packaging. She pointed out a trap door in the packaging room, which led to the cellar where employees were to go in the event of an air raid during the Second World War. She then proudly showed me the essence room, with the rows of old bottles containing the various mixtures and the old mixing table. There were various containers filled with the famous old mixtures – Camphor Menthol, Irish D – made from stalk not leaf, Kendal Brown and SP. Some were quite strong and pungent – all different for varied tastes.

Martin then showed me down into darkened rooms containing age-old black presses, reaching up towards the darkened ceiling, with belts and pulleys overhead. Separately in a cold press is the brown twist that is being compressed, five rounds of 500 gm twist in each metal cylinder. He next showed me the now motorised steam press in operation – this is how it was cooked.

He demonstrated how flake was made. The tobacco goes into small boxes, pressed overnight, cooked an hour, left overnight, then back into another press and then held for a month. Finally it is put into the old cutting machine to be cut. Shag is made at the new factory.

The company has now a foot in both worlds – old and new. They now have thirty-five on their staff: sales manager, reps, office staff and production and packing staff. Have a huge list of tobacco for sale, up-to-date equipment, a website and worldwide sales. There have been many roller coaster rides during the years, with changing conditions, the sad demise of heavy industry and mining shook the industry. The law is constantly changing. Duty was taken off snuff in 1978 but left on tobacco. Today they have to contend with the different changes brought in by the European Common Market together with bootleggers bringing duty free tobacco from abroad, both legally and illegally. This has hit sales. Selling cheaply in bars or to others in the black market has also affected tobacconist shops. The change in law at the beginning of 2003 stipulates that all tobacco and snuff products must carry a Government Health Warning. Later this year a ban on tobacco advertising comes into force – this will all have an adverse effect on sales. So the battle with tobacco, the whys and the wherefores continues into the twenty first century.

REFERENCES

1 Bingham, R. 1994. *Kendal – A Social History.* Cicerone Press
2 Curwen, J. F. 1900. *Kirkbie Kendall.* Titus Wilson, Kendal.
3 Cumbrian Record Office WRO/456, WDB 14/9
4 Somervell, J. 1930. *Water-Power Mills of South Westmorland.* Titus Wilson, Kendal.
5 Satchell, J. 2001. *Kendal's Canal.* Kendal Civic Society
6 Bulmer, T. F. 1884, *History, Topography and Directory of Westmorland.*
7 Kellys, 1897. *Directory of Cumberland and Westmorland.*
8 Parson and White, 1829 *History, Directory and Gazetteer of Cumberland and Westmorland.*
9 Holden's Triennial Directory, 4th ed. For 1804, 1806 and 1807
9 Wickham Legg, L. G. 1634. *A Relation of a Short Journey.*
10 Beckett, J. V. *Coal and Tobacco. The Lowthers and Economic Development of West Cumberland, 1660–1760.*
11 *An Illustrated Account of Kendal and Windermere c1900*
12 Atack, John, *The History of House of Samuel Gawith of Kendal 1792–1934.*
13 Edmondson, Ken, *The World of Snuff.*
14 Various articles in The Daily Telegraph, Guardian, Westmorland Gazette, Evening Mail, Lancashire Evening Post, Edgar Allen News, Cumbria Magazine and Cumbria Life.
15 Shepherd, C. W. 1963. *Snuff Yesterday & Today.* G. Smith & Sons, London.

If you have enjoyed this book you may also enjoy other books published by Helm Press.

'**A Westmorland Shepherd**' His life, poems and songs

'**Elephants On The Line**' Tales of a Cumbrian Railwayman (1947-95)

'**Dear Mr Salvin**' The story of the building of a 19th century Ulverston church

'**All In A Lifetime**' The story of a Dalesman as told to June Fisher

'**Hawkshead Revisited**" A Walk in time through Hawkshead

'**A Century of Heversham and Leasgill**' A walk in time through these old Westmorland villages

'**An Old Westmorland Garage**' The story behind Crabtree's of Kendal

'**Ambleside Remembered**' People and Places, Past and Present

'**Snagging Turnips and Scaling Muck**' The Women's Land Army in Westmorland

'**The Windermere Ferry**' History, Boats, Ferrymen & Passengers

'**Kendal Green**' A Georgian Wasteland Transformed

Helm Press
10 Abbey Gardens, Natland, Kendal, Cumbria LA9 7SP
Tel: 015395 61321
E-mail: HelmPress@natland.freeserve.co.uk